AF538831

PADMASAMBHAVA

THE GREAT INDIAN PANDIT

Neten Chokling Rinpoche

Series Editor: Aruna Vasudev

First published 2016

Hagiographies from various Tibetan texts and the well-known book *The Lotus Born-The Life Story of Padmasambhava*, Ranjung Yeshe Publications, were consulted for this book. The translation of the 'Sutra of Prediction in Magadha' is from *The Lotus Born-The Life Story of Padmasambhava*, Ranjung Yeshe Publications. Teachings of Padmasambhava are taken from the book *Advice from the Lotus Born*, Ranjung Yeshe Publications. The teaching called 'The Instruction of Pointing the Staff at the Old Man' is an extract from the book *Advice from the Lotus Born*, Ranjung Yeshe Publications.

Photograph Credits: Chokyi Palmo-pp iv-v, 1, 2, 3, 6, 12, 33, 63, 64, 74; Neten Chockling-pp viii, 13, 23, 25, 29, 37, 58; Matthieu Ricard-pp 30, 45; Shechen Archives-pp 61, 65, 66; p 51 courtesy Prof Lokesh Chandra; pp 7, 18, 67-68 used by the permission of Her Majesty Ashi Kesang Choeden Wangchuck. © 2012 Gatshel Publishing

ISBN 978-81-8328-465-3

Published by
Wisdom Tree
4779/23, Ansari Road
Darya Ganj, New Delhi-110 002
Ph.: 011-23247966/67/68
wisdomtreebooks@gmail.com

Printed in India

page ii
It is said that at seeing the statue in Samye monastery in Tibet, Padmasambhava remarked, 'It looks like me,' and then blessed it, saying, 'Now it is the same as me.' This is the only known photograph of this image. The photograph was taken by the late Queen Mother of Sikkim on her visit to Tibet before 1959.

CONTENTS

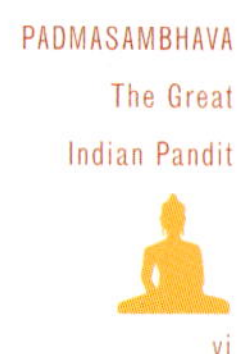

EDITOR'S NOTE

That India is the birthplace of Buddhism has long been acknowledged but in the country of its birth it almost disappeared. Today in India it is principally associated with Tibet. But why Tibet? How did this happen?

Although a very genuine interest in Buddhism is now spreading with astonishing rapidity around India and around the world, almost nothing is known of the great Indian masters who were responsible for the spread of Buddhism outside India. Who were these masters? Where did they come from? How and to which countries near and far were they the instruments for not only the spread but even the preservation of Buddhism?

The great, the 'Lotus-born' Padmasambhava, in the forgotten annals of history, was the first great revered master to be invited by the King of Tibet to teach and propagate Buddhism. His story, long-forgotten in India, is alive to the Buddhists of Tibet. It is a legend, it is a fairy tale, it had a profound impact on the Tibet of that ancient era when it was slowly fading away in the land of his birth.

To learn not only the story of his life, but to get a glimpse of what he taught, can have a profound impact on the reader today. As more and more Indians are rediscovering Buddhism and turning towards this deep yet essentially simple philosophy without any trimmings of idolatry, it seems to answer the need universally felt today to free ourselves from a way of life that is becoming increasingly destructive, both physically and emotionally.

To present the great masters and their teachings in a simple, easy-to-grasp manner, is a need that we have tried to fulfil through this series of books. To find the right author who would agree to write about the great guru Padmasambhava, was not an easy task. When my friend Bryan Mulvihill said he could ask Chockling Rinpoche to do it, I was stunned. I couldn't believe he would agree to do it. I had seen his film on Milarepa and was told he was planning to do one on Padmasambhava, it seemed like the perfect answer. I waited with bated breath for his reaction. When I was told he would do it, it was like a dream come true. And when the manuscript arrived, it was perfect. How could one ask for more. His utterly charming, gentle, very knowledgeable young wife, Choyang-la, came to Delhi a few times and sorted out problems like illustrations and clarifications. The result is a book that has the quality of easy to read, yet deeply illuminating. I hope you will enjoy it as much as I did.

I am deeply and eternally grateful to Dr Lokesh Chandra for his illuminating insights and the patience with which he bore with my questions and eagerness to learn over the past several years, and for his help in practical terms, with photographs and clarifications, for this hopefully ongoing series of books. Chokyi Palmo was very generous with giving some of her photographs for the books and Achal Kumar generously gave of his time and expertise in taking some expert quality photographs; Kshipra Simon was always ready when needed to take more photographs. Choyang-la, Ashok Wangdi, Bryan Mulvihill—all helped in a variety of ways to make this dream a reality.

—Aruna Vasudev
Series Editor

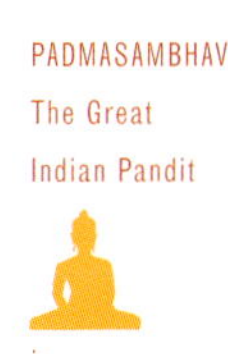

PREFACE

This book on Padmasambhava is a compilation of many hagiographies of the master. They are numerous in number and none of them contradict each other. There are hagiographies spoken by Padmasambhava and written down by his close student and confidante Yeshe Tsogyal and there are also those, which were written down by his other immediate disciples.

India is a land rich in Buddhist heritage. From Jammu and Kashmir to the southern state of Tamil Nadu, there are Buddhist indications of India's past. My aspiration is that this book on Padmasambhava will enrich the readers about their extraordinary lineage and make them feel proud of their past. It is also my aspiration that the Buddhist heritage of India is kept alive by the future generations.

As a Buddhist, I am very grateful to Aruna Vasudev for coming up with the idea for a series of books on Buddhist masters of Indian heritage. This will be of tremendous benefit for now and for the future. My appreciation also goes to Shobit Arya and Wisdom Tree for publishing this series of books.

—Neten Chockling

---

left
A *terma* statue of Padmasambhava. This is a *terma* revealed by the *terton* Sangay Lingpa (1340-1396).

PADMASAMBHAVA
THE GREAT INDIAN PANDIT

The Great Indian Pandit, whose kindness for Tibet is great,
The one born in a lotus, whose body is beyond birth and death.
Right now taming and subduing the rakshasas of the South West,
The precious one of Uddiyana, to you we pray!

This is an invocation to Padmasambhava, oft repeated throughout the land of Tibet. The opening words give the title he is famously known by, 'The Great Indian Pandit', whose largesse can never be measured.

Unfortunately, very little is known about this pandit today, not even in his homeland, when he seems to have such a palpable impact on the Tibetan masses and the Vajrayana Buddhists all over the world.

Yet, I personally feel all hope is not lost. The mighty sage, whom the Tibetans revere so much, has certainly not passed into oblivion in the subcontinent of his birth.

Nine years ago, I was at the Indian Museum in Kolkata. I was walking through the Gandhara

Padmasambhava holding a trident in the crook of his left arm and a *kapala* sits in his left hand. In his right hand at the level of his chest, he holds onto his 'dorje'—a vajra, symbolising indestructibility.

left
A statue of Padmasambhava overlooks *Tso Pema* (the Lotus Lake) in Rewalsar, HP. Legends talk of how he was taken captive by the local king and burnt alive but he miraculously turned the burning pyre into a lake. Today pilgrims come to *Tso Pema* from all over India and abroad.

Gallery when a particular statue caught my eye. I went closer to examine it; it was tagged simply 'Bodhisattva', with no name following the title. My curiosity piqued, I walked a little further, hoping to find more versions of this statue. Soon enough, I found another; this one was labelled 'Royal Bodhisattva'. The attire and jewellery adorning the statue were easily recognisable as representing royal descent. A most prominent moustache was the highlight of the regal face and I thought to myself excitedly, *This must be the Great Indian Pandit!* I rejoiced, thinking that here then was the long lost link to the rich heritage of the Vajrayana Buddhists, a link that would be so precious to innumerable Indians. This statue was indeed believed to be a true representation of the mysterious Padmasambhava—endorsed even by a few Tibetan masters—the enigmatic and much-revered Indian guru who introduced Buddhism to the Tibetans.

There are many hagiographies of Padmasambhava available today and none of them really contradict each other. Some are quite long, running into several pages, while others are rather short, pointing only to the major

Tibetan monasteries and hermitages are found in the vicinity of the Padmasambhava statue. There is also a cave associated with the master. One can often come across pilgrims circumambulating the lake and chanting the mantra of Padmasambhava.

commonly known events in his life. What I am about to recount here in this book is bits and pieces picked from various hagiographies as well as stories of liberation of his students. As a Vajrayana practitioner, I grew up listening to many biographical accounts, and as a young novice in the monastery, I was introduced to the *Padma Kathang*, a lengthy hagiography of Padmasambhava. We used to read it over and over to a point where we almost memorised the entire book! The Vajrayana Buddhists are advised to either read themselves or to commission others to read Padmasambhava's *namthar* (the Tibetan word for hagiography) for protection from sickness and obstacles in one's life. The moment someone is born, Padmasambhava's name is enunciated aloud for the well-being of the mother and child; as also, when someone is on his deathbed, he is reminded to keep Padmasambhava in his heart, for without a doubt, he will peacefully guide the consciousness in its onward journey. This is how Padmasambhava is very much an integral belief woven into the very fabric of every life.

In the *Sutra of Predictions in Magadha*, the Buddha foretells Padmasambhava's appearance:

> *I will pass away to eradicate the view of permanence.*
> *But twelve years from now, to clear away the view of nihilism,*
> *I shall appear from a lotus in the immaculate Lake Kosha*
> *As a noble son to please the king*
> *And turn the Dharma wheel of unexcelled essential meaning.*

These spoken words of the Buddha show that Padmasambhava did manifest within our human realm. He appeared in many different parts of the Indian subcontinent, including India, Pakistan, Bangladesh and the neighbouring lands of Afghanistan, Nepal, Bhutan, Sri Lanka, Tibet and China. But it is only in Tibetan Buddhism that his incarnation is unquestioningly accepted, where he continues to have a tremendous impact on its adherents. The information we have on Padmasambhava is drawn from Tibetan sources.

The story of Buddhism in India is like the story of any other religion. It has seen its share of ups and downs. The path of the Sutra was popularly practised and spread not only within the subcontinent

but also among its neighbouring lands such as Sri Lanka, Myanmar, Cambodia, Indonesia, Thailand, Vietnam and China, among other lands. This is one reason why we have many sources to cite when we talk about the Buddha. But the path of the Tantra, or the Secret Mantra path of the Vajrayana, was practised under much secrecy and only by a few initiates. It was never openly taught or practised. With the decline of Buddhism in India, the Tantra path, which was from the very beginning 'hidden', now went into complete hiding.

As prophesied by the Buddha, Padmasambhava is the 'Lord of the Secret Mantra'. It was this Secret Mantra, also known as Vajrayana, that Padmasambhava brought to Tibet in the eighth century AD. Tibet is the only land where Vajrayana truly flourished, where the lineage is alive and thriving, and it is solely thanks to the work of Padmasambhava that we have these teachings in the world today.

Padmasambhava was not an ordinary man. He was already an enlightened being who had come to our world to serve sentient beings. His birth in a lotus may seem unsettling to some. But no doubt, we have heard of miraculous births before—the baby Buddha emerging from the right side of his mother's body and baby Jesus born to a virgin mother.

Until as late as the seventeenth century AD, Tibetan pilgrims visited Swat valley or Uddiyana (in present-day Pakistan) in quest of Padmasambhava's birthplace. This pilgrimage halted entirely, perhaps because of the disappearance of Buddhism from the west of Ladakh. When active contact ceased, Uddiyana became a fabled land, shrouded in mystery and magic. The famous Tibetologist, Giuseppe Tucci, in his book, *Travels of Tibetan Pilgrims in the Swat Valley*, writes that Uddiyana was 'transformed into a fairyland, of which the geographical and historical reality faded and decayed'.

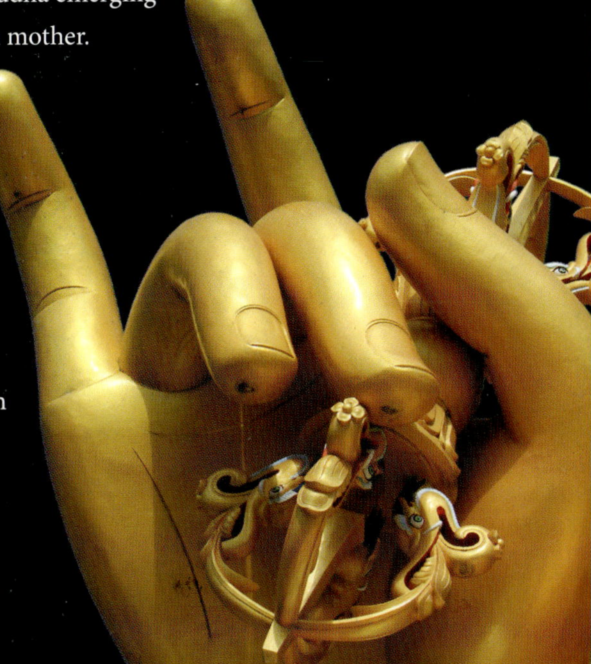

Padmasambhava carries the 'dorje'—vajra (in Sanskrit) in his right hand. The 'dorje' symbolises the qualities of being unconquerable, impregnable and indestructible.

TRISONG DUETSEN

THE STORY BEGINS

It is 809 AD, the year of the Ox. Trisong Duetsen is the sovereign, the thirty-eighth in a line of kings originating from a divine being hailing from India. The king has been engaged in continuous battle for many years, and under his commandership, Tibet's tract of land has expanded in every direction. The nation is at the height of her imperial power and neighbouring lands hold her in fear and apprehension.

The twenty-year-old king walks proudly around the battlefield. His men are rejoicing and celebrating yet another win—one more addition to the already vast dominion. As the men shout out cries of victory, the king sees the hunger in their eyes, the hunger for more land. His own eyes scan the horizon and settle on the towering mound of lifeless bodies, reaching into the skies. He feels the dead men staring back at him, their eyes hollow and empty, their vacant gaze piercing his heart. In the background, he hears the bellowing and regaling of his soldiers. And the stark contrast horrifies him. He feels a great wave of remorse wash over him, a sweeping sorrow for himself and his men.

Something stirs within the young king and a deep sadness takes root in his heart. At the zenith of his power, a noble aspiration forms in his mind. The thought germinates, to revitalise Buddhism, and

left
Padmasambhava as the main figure is surrounded by his eight manifestations. These eight manifestations are the eight principal forms assumed by him at different stages in his life. In actuality, they are all the same but appear and manifest according to the different needs of the beings.

he declares, 'I must cause the holy Dharma to spread and flourish. For this, I shall construct a temple that shall house the Three Jewels and be an object of devotion and veneration.'

Returning to his palace, Trisong Duetsen acts with alacrity. The courtier, Yeshe Shunu (Jnana Kumara, in Sanskrit), who can speak Sanskrit is summoned. With two attendants, the envoy of the Tibetan emperor sets off with great urgency for India, bearing gifts of gold dust for the abbot of Nalanda.

Shantarakshita

The Tibetan envoys headed by Yeshe Shunu arrive in India at the glorious Nalanda, the famed university and monastic centre for Buddhist studies. Assuming the highest priority, they request an audience with Shantarakshita, the abbot, and convey to him the urgency of the message from the Tibetan king who sent them. The abbot accepts the invitation to make the perilous journey. Something important is to take place—a plan conjured many hundreds of years ago in another lifetime.

The Indian monk and the Tibetans slowly make their way past the hot plains of India. They pass by palm trees whose branches sway in the breezy nights, and in the early dawn, they wake before the sound of the cuckoo's 'koo-ooo' envelops the air. The frolicking peacocks performing their ritual dance in the forest clearing give way to the mountain goats sprinting and darting from one rocky crag to the next. As the men climb higher into the mist, the air becomes brittle and thin. The travellers cross paths with the majestic snow leopards who walk elegantly past them, silently, as if in meditation. Slowly and steadily, they make their way up towards the highest plateau of the mighty Himalayas.

Trisong Duetsen was Tibet's second great Dharma king. His forefather, the emperor Songtsen Gampo was the first to introduce Buddhism in his domain. He sent his most trusted and intelligent minister to India to study the language and in turn created the first Tibetan alphabet. Songtsen Gampo married a Buddhist princess from China and the Buddhist princess Bhrikuti Devi from Nepal. These two Buddhist queens from the neighbouring lands would influence Tibet in great ways.

Before the arrival of Padmasambhava, Tibet was a wild land. The Tibetans were great warriors and were feared for their barbaric ways across the vast valleys and steppes. Under Trisong Duetsen, Tibet stretched its domain beyond the 'prosperity and protector' temples built by Songtsen Gampo. It is into this Tibet that the Nalanda abbot is invited with the greatest show of gratitude and indebtedness by the Tibetan emperor.

On his arrival, Shantarakshita is given a warm welcome by Trisong Duetsen at his palace at Red Rock. The Tibetan king presents to the abbot a variety of gifts and humbly requests, 'Great Master, I wish to construct a temple for the Buddha, the Dharma and the Sangha.' The Indian abbot assures the king, 'Noble king, I will do my best.' And the construction of the temple is discussed.

The Play of the *Yul-lhas*

It is 810 AD, the year of the Iron Tiger. A year has passed since the noble aspiration dawned in Trisong Duetsen's heart, and Tibet embarks on her most important undertaking. An excited Trisong Duetsen inaugurates by making the first dig with a golden hoe as his courtiers watch from all sides. After the earth is touched by his noble wish, Shantarakshita then steps forward and by virtue of his contemplation, garners the strength of his *bodhichitta* and offers the noble work for the benefit of all beings.

The construction work begins as men and beasts of burden slowly proceed inward from the periphery, carrying mud and stones. The king excitedly watches until the sun sinks behind the mountains. Early in the morning, there is a commotion among the men. The mud and stones gathered for the foundation have disappeared. The men look all around and are speechless. Nevertheless, they decide to begin work again. In the straw and jute bags that sit on their backs, the beasts bring in the materials for building. And the men who lead them also carry a share on their backs. The work progresses slowly and the foundation of the building comes alive.

Early one morning, as the king is doing his rounds of the building site, a big shock is laid in front of his eyes. All that was built before is gone, leaving no proof of any previous infrastructure. One of the labourers exclaims, 'No human could have done this in a single night!' The king is aghast. He remains silent for a few seconds before he musters up the courage to command his people, 'We have to carry on!'

In all four directions, the men start rolling the boulders towards the site. Some men bring in the mud and stones on their backs and the animals trudge along slowly with parcels on their backs. Nearing dusk, Trisong Duetsen inspects the construction, and although he is happy, a feeling of worry pervades his heart. The foundation has been laid and the men are erecting the walls. As the stars fill the vast open sky, the Tibetans return home, happy and satisfied after a hard day's work.

Come morning, the king comes to inspect the site. And what he sees is a wrecked foundation of the building in the middle of the plain, with a thick curtain of dust hanging all around. He walks around the pile of dust and rubble. Picking up a handful of dirt off the ground, he hurls it in the air. The king's men and the Indian abbot watch quietly as the young king looks towards the mountains, his eyes brimming with tears. As the ministers look helplessly towards the king, the Indian monk walks over and empathetically pats the young man on the back. Trisong Duetsen falls to his knees and breaks down. 'What my men build by day is being destroyed by nightfall. How will the temple be accomplished?' There is a note of pain and discontentment in his voice. With compassion, the monk consoles him, 'Don't lose heart! All will be fine.'

The young king questions the monk, 'Don't I have sufficient merit? Are the abbot's blessings not strong enough?' The monk shakes his head and replies, 'It is not that the king doesn't have sufficient merit or that my blessings are not strong enough. The malicious spirits are creating obstacles and they are not responding to my compassion. Only by wrathful means can they can be tamed and there is only one person who can perform this task.' The abbot's words enliven the dispirited king who asks at once, 'Who is he?' The monk replies, 'Even the Buddha foretold his appearance. His miraculous birth from a lotus was prophesied by the Buddha himself in the Nirvana Sutra.' The king looks at the abbot in anticipation, 'What is his name?' With great reverence then, the abbot brings his palms together and says, 'He is Padmasambhava.'

right
Padmasambhava is known for his wrathful yet compassionate nature in taming the minds of sentient beings.

UDDIYANA
BIRTH
AND
RENUNCIATION

The country of Uddiyana, *O-rgyan* in Tibetan, is nestled in the Swat valley. If you look for Swat Valley on the map, you will find it in Pakistan. King Indrabhuti, the ruler of Uddiyana, was without an heir. On the advice of seers and astrologers, the pious king emptied his treasury, giving away his wealth to the needy of his kingdom. Yet no heir was born to him.

In order to restore the treasury, the king decides to go to the Jewel Island. He boards his sea vessel and sails across the ocean, knowing that he could keep up his generosity and the gods would, in return, grant him a boon in the form of an heir. Returning from the Jewel Island, the king and his retinue are astounded to see a huge multicoloured lotus of incomparable beauty. Sitting on the pollen bed of the lotus, they see what appears to be an eight-year-old boy. The king and his courtiers marvel at this spectacular sight.

The king asks the boy who he is and where he comes from. In response, the boy answers, 'I come from nowhere. I have no father. I have no mother. I have no family and I don't belong to a clan.' Thinking that the gods have finally heard his prayers, an overjoyed Indrabhuti lifts the wondrous boy and places him on a silken cushion. He is named Padmasambhava, Sanskrit for 'Lotus Born'.

The lotus born prince then receives princess Luminous Bearer of Singala as his bride. He enjoys the company of his beautiful and intelligent wife and excels in all the sports of the kingdom.

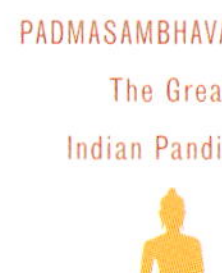

Throughout the land, he is loved and held in awe for his beauty and brilliance. A doting father, a beautiful wife and a wealthy kingdom encircle him and he delights in the luxury of his mundane life. Five years pass by in this manner until one day, the Buddha Vajrasattva manifests in front of him and reminds him of his purpose in life. The prince realises that ruling the kingdom was not the purpose he was born to serve. Leaving behind his loving family and his father's kingdom, he renounces his worldly life. Assuming the guise of a wandering ascetic, the Uddiyana prince sets off from his kingdom in the southern direction.

This life is crossed in a brief moment, but samsara is endless. What will you do in the next life? Also, the length of this life is not guaranteed: the time of death lies uncertain, and like a convict taken to the scaffold, you draw closer to death with each step.

All beings are impermanent and die. Haven't you heard about the people who died in the past? Haven't you seen any of your relatives die? Don't you notice that we grow old? And still, rather than practising the Dharma, you forget about past grief. Rather than dreading future misery, you ignore the suffering of the lower realms.

Chased by temporary circumstances, tied by the rope of dualistic fixation, exhausted by the river of desire, caught in the web of samsaric existence, held captive by the tight shackles of karmic ripening—even when the tidings of the Dharma reach you, you still cling to diversions and remain careless. Is it that death doesn't happen to people like you? I pity all sentient beings who think in this way!

page 13
Next to the Maratika Cave, Eastern Nepal. Prayer flags flutter in the wind carrying the mantra of Padmasambhava. These prayer flags bearing the mantras of different Buddhas and bodhisattvas are found in all the areas of Buddhist worship. Here in Rewalsar, which is associated with Padmasambhava, the prayer flags contain his mantra.

CHARNEL GROUNDS AND GURUS

The yogi prince arrives at Sitavana, one of the most terrifying charnel grounds, where the spirits of the dead created apparitions even in broad daylight. At nightfall, predators roamed side by side with the spirits, hungry and looking for food. In the dead of the night, as the predators howled in hunger, the spirits howled in loneliness. Padmasambhava settles here and five years pass by. Unknown to the common man, he instructs the charnel ground *dakini*s, extraordinary women of mundane and supramundane powers who are on the spiritual path, on the highest form of meditation.

The followers of Padmasambhava often visit Sitavana, located near Bodh Gaya. Sitavana is counted as one of the Eight Great Charnel Grounds frequented by Padmasambhava during his sojourns. It is known to be an intimidating and frightening place, impossible for unworthy people to approach. It is in these terrifying charnel grounds that Padmasambhava taught his human and non-human disciples.

In order to pay obeisance to the Buddha, Padmasambhava travels to the nearby town of Gaya. There, in front of the Vajra Seat where the Buddha attained enlightenment, the young yogi pays tribute by offering his praises and reverence. Hundreds of monks materialise offering flowers, fruits and prostrations to the revered seat. Hundreds of yogis too appear, offering their praises and prostrations. Then these apparitions transform back into Padmasambhava.

A native who witnesses the whole event approaches the yogi and asks, ‘You pay such magnificent

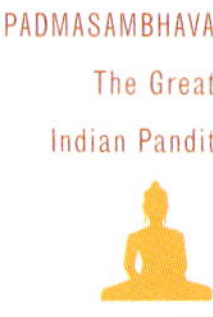

obeisance to the Enlightened One's seat. Whose disciple are you?' Padmasambhava responds, 'I have no father and I have no mother. I have no teacher nor master. I have no caste and I have no name. I am a self-appeared Buddha.' The native is taken aback and says in disbelief, 'Someone who displays miracles without a teacher must be a demon!' And he backs away from Padmasambhava apprehensively.

Though he has spoken the truth, Padmasambhava realises that for him to benefit people, they need to place their confidence and trust in him. So he takes to learning and studies the Five Sciences, the sutras and the tantras from the learned and accomplished siddhas of the subcontinent, who bestow upon him the empowerment (*Abhisheka*, in Sanskrit) of the tantras with their instructions explained. Studying under several male and female preceptors, Padmasambhava goes through the process of hearing, reflecting and meditating on the instructions and empowerments that he receives from his masters. These masters include Manjushrimitra of Magadha, Nagarjuna and Buddhaguhya of India, Vimalamitra and Prabhahasti of Western India, Hungkara of Nepal, Dhana Sanskrita, Shantigarbha, Prahevajra and Guhyachandra of Uddiyana, and Shri Singha of China.

From the eight *Vidyadhara*s or knowledge holders, he receives the Eight Sadhana Teachings on the eight chief tutelary deities of Mahayoga and their corresponding tantras and sadhanas.

- Manjushrimitra—Transmission of the Yamantaka Tantra
- Nagarjuna—Transmission of the Hayagriva Tantra
- Vimalamitra—Transmission of the Mahotarra Tantra
- Prabhahasti—Transmission of the Vajrakilaya Tantra
- Hungkara—Transmission of the Vishuddha Tantra
- Dhana Sanskrita—Transmission of the liberating sorcery of Mother deities
- Guhyachandra—Transmission of mundane worship
- Shantigarbha—Transmission of maledictory fierce mantras

From the master Garab Dorje (Prahevajra) Padmasambhava receives the transmission on the heart essence of the Great Perfection (*Mahasandhi*, in Sanskrit). The master Sangay Sangwa (Buddhaguhya)

transmits to him the Guhyagarbha Tantra and the master Shri Singha bestows on him the Mahotarra Heruka Tantra as well as teachings on the Great Perfection.

Similarly, he is empowered many times by his female masters. At the Sitavana charnel ground, the wisdom *dakini* Lekyi Wangmo (Karmeshvari, Karma Indranila, in Sanskrit) teaches him the Assemblage of Sugatas. At the charnel ground of Sosaling, to the south of Uddiyana, he practises yogic discipline and is empowered and blessed by the *dakini* Sustainer of Peace. At Rugged Grove charnel ground in Uddiyana, he has a vision of the wisdom *dakini* Vajra Varahi who empowers him. While at the charnel ground of Joyful Grove in Sahor, he is empowered and blessed by the *dakini* Tamer of Mara. In the charnel ground of Sandal Grove, the wisdom *dakini* Sangwa Yeshe (Guhyajyana), appearing in the form of the nun Kungamo, empowers him externally as Buddha Amitabha, internally as Avalokiteshvara, and secretly as the wrathful tantric deity, Hayagriva, the Horse-headed One.

Under the guidance of his teachers, Padmasambhava displays the ability to cut through ignorance with the sword of wisdom. He serves the doctrine of the Buddha at the Vajra Seat for many years until his departure to Sahor, when Mahapandit Vimalamitra takes over the responsibility of guarding the Buddha Dharma.

It doesn't matter whether your act of giving is as small as a single sesame seed; if you give with compassion and *bodhichitta* you achieve hundredfold merit. If you give without the *bodhichitta* resolve, your merit will not increase even if you give away horses and cattle.

---

page 18
Padmasambhava as a wall painting. He is seen wearing his special hat and a *khatvanga* (trident) in the crook of his left arm. In his right hand is the 'dorje' and his left hand holds a *kapala* with blessed amrita. His face expresses wrathful compassion.

SAHOR
INDIA

The king of Sahor had a daughter by the name of Mandarava. Right from a young age, she was different from others and showed signs of being an extraordinary being. So when she comes of age to be wed, many suitors arrive from the neighbouring lands, but Mandarava shows no curiosity about these men who have come from far and near as she has already given herself to the Dharma. Deep down the Sahor king is worried lest he angers any of the suitors if his daughter refuses them. He approaches the princess about her impending marriage and tells her that she can choose as her heart desires. But Mandarava has no desire for she knows that marriage will tie her down to samsara and its trappings.

One day, weary with the constant badgering by her suitors, the princess leaves the palace through a secret door. Walking eastwards with her attendant, she comes to a quiet spot. There, in an emotional state of being overwhelmed with samsara, she casts off the silk clothing that covers her body and unties the ornaments that adorn her. She exclaims, 'Except for the Buddha's teaching, I have no other attachments.' The princess crushes her ornaments with a rock and scatters them in front of her. In a stirring tone, she makes a heartfelt plea, 'May my thoughts follow the path of the Dharma! May I not be sent away as a bride!' She shreds to pieces her clothes and tosses them in the four directions. Again she grieves strongly, 'May I be free from the bondages of a life of the eight worldly concerns!' A scream of agony of great power and intensity issues from her chest. She starts pulling her hair and scratches her face so that no admirer will accept her. Her attendant quickly goes to the king and reports to him the incident she has witnessed in the forest.

A distressed father responds to his daughter's condition by gathering all the kings and their ambassadors at his palace. He presents them with gifts and offerings and sends them away respectfully, affirming that his daughter has chosen no one but the Dharma. The men go back to their lands satisfied that none acquired Mandarava's hand. In the meantime, Mandarava is ordained into the spiritual path along with many of her female attendants. The king makes a special palace for his daughter and her attendants with the strictest orders that no men be allowed inside.

Padmasambhava arrives in the kingdom of Sahor knowing that the Sahor princess, his karmically destined disciple, would be found there. One day, while Mandarava and her attendants are disporting in the outdoors, they come across Padmasambhava. The princess feels a great sense of trust and confidence towards the yogi and she invites him to her palace to impart his teachings. During one of these teaching sessions, a cowherd passing by her palace hears a man's voice. The cowherd is curious as no men are allowed inside Mandarava's palace; this was a revelation! He quickens his pace towards the village, full of tales to tell. Rumours quickly start going around and the news eventually reaches the king's ear.

The king is enraged as no royal daughter of his will associate with any mendicant. On the command of the king, the soldiers surround Mandarava's palace even as Padmasambhava is giving instructions to the princess. Ignoring Mandarava's plea, the king's men take the master captive and tie him to a stake on a mound of heaped wood. Oil of a hundred thousand seeds is poured and the pyre is set afire. The princess is thrown into the dungeon as a punishment.

From the window of his palace, the Sahor king looks up into the dark skies. For seven long days and nights, thick black smoke billows up into the skies, keeping the kingdom in the dark shadows. Intrigued, the king climbs into his carriage and commands his retinue to follow him to investigate the strange phenomenon. On reaching the spot, the king is surprised to see the mendicant still alive,

sitting on a lotus in the middle of a beautiful lake. Remnants of the fire are seen at the periphery of the lake. Surrounding him is a throng of *dakini*s and devis, cleansing Padmasambhava and offering him various delights. From the sky above, Indra and Brahma with their entourages of devas and other celestial beings are showering flowers and praises on Padmasambhava.

As the king watches in amazement, the warmth of the embers and cinders alights gently on his face, bringing him back to the present. He is filled with a deep sense of remorse for his misconduct towards Padmasambhava. Asking for forgiveness and wishing to demonstrate his grief over his earlier action, the king unbridles his royal horses from his carriage. He invites the yogi into the carriage and pulls it himself. Arriving at the palace, the king quickly commands his guards to release the princess from her prison. With great remorse and faith, the king requests teachings from Padmasambhava for himself and his entire kingdom.

Among the five main consorts of Padmasambhava, Mandarava, the Bengali princess of the Sahor royal house and the Tibetan princess, Yeshe Tsogyal of the Karchen clan stand out for their contribution towards the Dharma. After meeting Padmasambhava and receiving teachings from him, Mandarava is sent to many places to teach the Dharma and carry out her enlightened activities. At one point, Padmasambhava tells her to travel to Mt Kailash in Tibet to bury certain terma *or treasure teachings. Using the power of speed-walking, she quickly reaches the mountain but the native spirits of Mt Kailash try their best to ward her off with their magic creations. Transforming herself into the* dakini *Uma Devi, she consorts with Mahadeva, the guardian of the mountain. She confers the secret empowerment upon him and then hands over the responsibility of the treasures into his care.*

---

page 23
Maratika Cave, Eastern Nepal. One descends down the stairs and enters the Maratika Cave. Here Padmasambhava stayed for three months meditating on Amitayus, the Buddha of Boundless Life. It is here that the Sahor princess accompanies her master. Both master and student are blessed by Buddha Amitayus.

MARATIKA CAVE
NEPAL

Mandarava and Padmasambhava travel north towards the Himalayas. At the cave of Maratika in Eastern Nepal, the master and his student disclose the mandala of Buddha Amitayus and perform the practice of mastery over life. After three months, the Buddha of Boundless Life, Amitayus, appears in person. He confers empowerment upon them and blesses them to be inseparable from him. Padmasambhava and the Indian princess attain the Vajra Body, the 'invincible body' transcending birth and death.

Returning from Maratika cave, Padmasambhava and Mandarava go to Uddiyana. There, he teaches his father, King Indrabhuti, and turns the wheel of Dharma, establishing the entire kingdom on the path of the Vajrayana. The master and student travel to many places while establishing the Dharma and putting people and kingdoms on the path of enlightenment. They also visit charnel grounds and teach the inhabitants occupying these terrifying sites, installing them as Dharma Guardians, the protectors of the Dharma.

In India, it is not surprising to hear of yogis who are said to be above 100 years of age. Even in Himachal Pradesh where I live, there is a yogi who is said to be a little over 100 years old but he still looks young and radiant. Every morning he comes out and those who go to seek his darshan can see him during his morning ritual of sitting in the sun. Some say that he uses the sun's energy to prolong his life. We have something called the chulen, *a method where one uses the elements from nature to nourish the body. There might be some who think that if Padmasambhava was born some years after the Buddha's passing away (as prophesied by the Buddha), then how can he be alive and active in Tibet in the eighth or ninth century. The mind being the creator of all that is perceived, it is possible to conquer ageing and it should not be difficult to accept that.*

THE SEVEN-LINE INVOCATION

While practising at the Jhalandhara charnel ground, an event unfolds at the Vajra Seat that would require Padmasambhava's help. Four powerful *tirthikas* have approached the Vajra Seat from the four directions. With five hundred followers standing behind each of them, the non-Buddhist extremists instigate a challenge. They lay the rules that should one lose, he should embrace the faith of the winning side. These four men were adherents of the Extreme View (eternalism and nihilism) as opposed to the Middle Path of the Buddhist pandits.

The four gate-keeping pandits at the Vajra Seat and all the other pandits are deeply concerned. They know that they can win in debate but cannot match the contest of magical powers. As the Buddhists worry and ponder among themselves for an answer, a blue-tinged woman appears. She says, 'Invite my brother and you will win.' They ask her who her brother is. She answers, 'My brother is Padmasambhava and he is practising in the charnel ground of Jhalandhara.' The pandits look to each other with hope and optimism. One of them replies, 'But how do we invite him?' The mysterious woman answers, 'Call him by this supplication and it will lure him here:

> *Hung. On the northwest border of the country of Uddiyana,*
> *On the anthers of a lotus flower,*
> *You attained the marvelous supreme siddhi,*

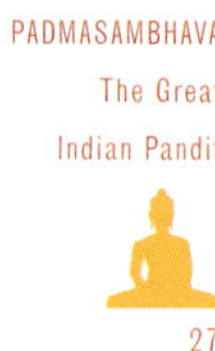

Renowned as the Lotus Born.
Surrounded by a retinue of many dakinis,
Following you, I will reach accomplishment.
Please come and bestow your blessings.
GURU PADMA SIDDHI HUNG.

The pandits start chanting the supplication.

Far away from the Vajra Seat in the Jhalandhara charnel ground, Padmasambhava hears the invocation.

At the break of dawn, he arrives at the Vajra Seat. As the sun rises, the Buddhists and the non-Buddhist extremists begin the debate. The Buddhists emerge as victors and the five hundred pandits surrounding Padmasambhava rejoice in their victory in both the dialectic of logic and magic. In the midst of the celebrations, the *tirthika*s flare up in fury and fly up in the air. Padmasambhava directs the menacing scorpion mudra at them and starts spinning a wheel of fire on his finger and flings it towards them. The *tirthika*s fly in different directions and are never to be heard of again. Their followers who are left behind embrace the Buddhist teachings. At the place of the Buddha's enlightenment, the conch of the Dharma is blown to sound in all the directions. To show their gratitude, the pandits enthrone and shower Padmasambhava with praises.

It is extremely difficult to obtain a human body. Having obtained it, only a few people hear the name of the Buddha. After hearing it, it is extremely rare that someone feels faith. And even feeling faith once, after entering the Dharma many people like stubborn beasts break their *samayas* (vows that create a bond between a disciple and a guru) and precepts and head downhill. Seeing these sentient beings, the bodhisattvas despair, and I, Padmakara, grieve.

PADMASAMBHAVA'S NAME IS UTTERED IN TIBET

The young king, Trisong Duetsen, listens in awe as Shantarakshita describes Padmasambhava's life story. Excitedly the king asks, 'Where is he right now?' The abbot's answer is quick, 'At the moment, he is at the cave of Asura in the southern land of Nepal. You must invite him to Tibet!'

Immediately, five Tibetans are chosen by the king himself, furnished with gold dust as gifts for Padmasambhava, and dispatched with a desperate urgency to the land lying to the south of Tibet.

In the Wish-Fulfilling Tree, *a hagiography of Padmasambhava, it is said that actually Shantarakshita was capable of taming the spirits and devas of Tibet. But because he knew the importance of the three of them coming together for the Dharma, the abbot advised the king to invite Padmasambhava, whose wrathful wisdom was needed to subdue the spirits of the land.*

---

page 25
Wall painting of Padmasambhava in a temple above Dhankar monastery in Spiti valley. This particular photo was taken in 2006 and the wall over which this painting was done was crumbling. There is an urgent need to restore these precious murals, which are part of many temples and monasteries spread over the Himalayas, as these are a part of our human heritage.

ASURA CAVE
NEPAL

At the upper cave of Yanglesho, Padmasambhava discloses the mandala of the nine-faced glorious Vishuddha Heruka to the Nepalese princess, Shakyadevi. Finding his presence in the valley a great disturbance, the native spirits of Nepal and India create havoc. Rain stops falling from the skies and the parched land yields no crop resulting in famine, disease and death of men and animals. Padmasambhava realises that the local deities are trying to hinder him from the accomplishment of his Mahamudra practice and in order to restore peace and well-being of the natives, the only solution lies in wrathfully taming and subduing the haughty spirits. Requesting his former master, Prabhahasti, in India, for a skillful method to revert and repel the hindrances, Padmasambhava dispatches two of his disciples to India.

In the villages around Asura cave, the mound of animal carcasses grows higher. Men, women and children, thin and dry as a twig, sit under their

left
Pilgrims pray to Padmasambhava at the Asura Cave, Pharping/ Yanglesho, Nepal. Here in the cave of Asura, Padmasambhava meditated on the wrathful deities Vajrakilaya and Vishuddha. After being blessed by the vision of the deities, he subdues the hostile spirits of the land and appoints them as guardians of the Buddha's teachings.

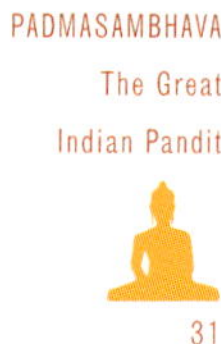

thatched roofs, gawking, their eyes bulging out of their sockets. In the meantime, in India, the two Nepalese disciples have arrived at Master Prabhahasti's place. Choosing from among many sections of the Kilaya teachings, the master selects the sadhanas meant for subduing obstructive forces.

Approximately forty minutes from Kathmandu is the town of Pharping. Here at the upper cave of Yanglesho called Asura, the Himalayan Buddhists following Vajrayana visit to offer butter lamps and prayers. As with other Padmasambhava sites, there is a non-stop inflow of pilgrims from the entire Himalayan belt. A yearly influx of people from Tibet, Ladakh, Himachal Pradesh, Bhutan and Sikkim among other regions takes place here. At least once a year, the various communities of Buddhists dwelling in the Kathmandu valley as well as the mountain-dwelling Buddhists make the trip to Asura cave to reconnect with him.

Back in Asura cave, a sudden burst of lightning lights up Padmasambhava's dark cave. Big droplets of water fall from the skies and down below, the villagers are heard singing and shouting with joy. As the parched earth is moistened, the land starts breathing once more, giving out vapour and sprouting greenery in abundance.

In the midst of this exultation, the Nepalese disciples arrive at Asura cave, carrying the load of palm leaf texts. The secret mantra of the deity Vajrakilaya resonates and reverberates faintly. They hand over the texts to Padmasambhava with the words, 'Master Prabhahasti's advice is that the practice of Vajrakilaya will help.' Padmasambhava accepts the texts with great reverence and says, 'On entering the border of this land, these precious texts have quelled the obstacles.'

With all hurdles cleared for the natives as well as for his spiritual practice, Padmasambhava has a vision of the glorious Vishuddha and the Vajrakilaya deities. He then composes and performs a combined sadhana of Vishuddha and Vajrakilaya and accomplishes the Mahamudra practice. At various times of the day, the haughty male and female spirits of the land come and offer the core of their lives to him. Padmasambhava binds them under oath and appoints them guardians of the Dharma, especially of the Vajrakilaya teachings.

---

page 30
A footprint left by Padmasambhava. Bodily prints of Padmasambhava are found in Tibet, India, Nepal, Bhutan and Sikkim. Many of these are kept as sacred objects in temples, monasteries and in certain cases with private individuals.

TIBET

Padmasambhava's Journey to Tibet

While at Asura cave, Padmasambhava is visited by the Dharma Guardians who appeal to him, 'Five envoys of the Tibetan king are coming to meet you but they are exhausted. Master, please go and meet them at the border.' Even though in India there was the danger of the *tirthika*s' view overtaking the land, the auspicious and prophesied time for Tibet had arrived.

Hearing of the master's plan to depart for Tibet, the native *dakini*s of Nepal come to see Padmasambhava. With great sadness, the goddesses speak. 'We hear that you will be going to the Northern land of snow. Please do not leave!' The *dakini*s implore him to stay but Padmasambhava has already made up his mind, 'I have to go this time.'

Earlier, over the border, in Tibet, the *yul-lha*s or the native spirits of the land get irritated and furious over the imminent arrival of the foreign master. 'No foreigner can come in with his foreign views,' they claim. 'This is our domain!'

The five Tibetan envoys brave the harsh elements of the Tibetan plateau. They walk the endless stretch of the earth, battling against dust storms, snowstorms and icy wind. The frozen mountains piercing the deep blue skies loom in front of the Tibetans, challenging them to scale their heights. As the men

brave the physical and the mental hardships, the malevolent devas and spirits of Tibet conjure up various tricks and magic to discourage them.

It takes almost three months for the Tibetans to reach the border on the southern land of Nepal. On reaching the vast plain of Mangyul, they look around for any sight of natives. As they talk among themselves about how to recognise Padmasambhava, they see a yogi with a *khatvanga*, a trident, walking in the far distance. The Tibetans rush up to him. The chief of the envoys asks the yogi, 'We are looking for Padmasambhava. Do you know him?' Now even though Padmasambhava knew who they were, he pretends ignorance and asks the chief, 'Where are you coming from?' The envoy replies, 'We are sent by the Tibetan king Trisong Duetsen.' The yogi smiles broadly and says, 'Three months ago, the guardians of the Buddha Dharma requested me to meet you here. What took you so long?'

In a flurry the emissaries prostrate at Padmasambhava's feet. The chief envoy quickly takes out the bags of gold dust from their luggage. He offers them to the yogi who, without any warning, scatters the gold dust in the air. As the gold dust mingles with the sand of Mangyul, Padmasambhava asks the dumbstruck Tibetans, 'Is it agonising to see your king's precious gold go to waste?' The Tibetans are shocked at such eccentric behaviour. They do not know what to do. The yogi then grabs a handful of soil from the ground and starts filling the folds of the envoys' clothes with it. The men are astounded as to what he will do next. 'Is this what you were grieving for?' asks Padmasambhava. The men peer into their pockets. Along with the gold dust, there are other precious stones. They gasp at the miracle shown by the yogi. 'I don't need gold. For me, all appearances are gold,' says Padmasambhava. The Tibetans' trust and confidence in Padmasambhava is strengthened.

Padmasambhava's departure for Tibet was seen as India losing its precious gem of the Vajrayana, which was heavily guarded at the Vajra Seat. It is said that around the time of his departure, there were, in India, some masters who dreamt unusual dreams. One such dream was that of the sun and moon arising together in the North. Yet another master dreamt of many flowers blooming in the North. It is said that one could hear the dakinis *of India frantically and sadly lamenting Padmasambhava's departure.*

left
Padmasambhava flanked by the Tibetan princess Yeshe Tsogyal (to his left) and the Indian princess Mandarava (to his right). He is seen sitting in a big lotus sprouting from a lake. His two female students are also seen sitting in lotus flowers. In the sky above Padmasambhava is Buddha Amitabha who is red in colour.

Back in Tibet, Trisong Duetsen is thrilled to hear news of the envoys' safe passage to the South. He now waits eagerly for Padmasambhava to arrive in Tibet. But in the South, at the Nepal-Tibet border, the various *yul-lha*s of Nepal and Tibet were conspiring together to pose danger and threat to the group.

The party arrives at a mountain pass at the upper end of Mangyul. The *yul-lha* of the area tries to create obstacles. She disguises herself as two mountains and tries to crush Padmasambhava and the Tibetans, but the yogi is quick. Fast as lightning, Padmasambhava strikes the mountain with his *khatvanga* and the *yul-lha* screams loudly, coming down head first, her eyes wide and disconcerted. She asks for his forgiveness and pledges her life to the protection of the Buddha Dharma. Padmasambhava accepts her submission and the men resume their journey.

Descending into a heavenly plain, an endless stretch of barren landscape, the shattering sound of a thunderclap freezes the Tibetans in their tracks. With nowhere to hide in the vast plain, they squat with their hands over their heads. A little further ahead of the Tibetans, Padmasambhava is seen holding up a mirror in the air. The lightning strikes again but he is quick enough to place the mirror in the direction of the lightning. On striking the mirror, the lightning is rendered powerless. Silence sweeps across the entire plain for a few seconds. Suddenly, a woman appears out of nowhere and runs towards a nearby lake. Padmasambhava commands her to stop but she quickly dives into the lake and disappears. Using the scorpion mudra, Padmasambhava visualises the lake as a mass of fire. In a few seconds, the lake begins to boil and a loud shriek fills the desolate plain. The woman emerges from the lake, her whole body covered in boils, her skin falling off the bones. She withers and bawls in pain. The Tibetans watch in horror as the woman crawls out of the lake and tries to escape but Padmasambhava's wrath is quick.

He hurls his vajra towards her and it hits her right eye. She falls down, blood oozing out of the eye. The *yul-lha* cries, 'I shall not harm anymore! Please, spare me!' Pieces of skin fall off her body and the bitter cold wind bites into her exposed flesh, making her twist in pain. She loses consciousness for a split second, then comes back to life. Padmasambhava demands, 'Are you giving me your word

of truth?' The *yul-lha* nods her head, 'We may be malevolent spirits but when we give an oath of allegiance, we are unwavering! I accept the Buddha's Dharma!' Padmasambhava blesses her and says, 'From today onwards, you are a Dharma Guardian. You will guard the teachings of the Buddha and its adherents.'

Further into Tibet, the group comes across a big white yak, the size of a mountain, standing in their way. Its nostrils flared, the huge beast breathes heavily and makes a roaring sound. It stares angrily at the group, stabbing the air sharply and violently with its horns. The Tibetans cower behind Padmasambhava for protection. The yak takes a formidable stance and charges towards the men but Padmasambhava catches the yak by the nose, wielding the hook mudra. He then binds the middle using the lasso mudra, shackles the legs using the chain mudra and hits him using the bell mudra. Immediately, the voice of a young boy is heard coming from the yak, pleading for forgiveness. Padmasambhava stops striking the animal and a young boy quickly releases himself from Padmasambhava's grip. The Tibetans are awestruck; their confidence in the yogi is reinforced. They rejoice that the foreign master their king has invited is going to be of help to Tibet after all.

These are just a few stories of the taming and subduing of the yul-lhas *by Padmasambhava. Throughout the trip, starting from the Nepal border all the way to central Tibet, where the Tibetan king was waiting for him, Padmasambhava not only tamed and subdued the spirits but also appointed them as Dharma Guardians, with the responsibility of protecting the Buddha's teachings. Today, the native* yul-lhas *of Tibet are Buddhists. Before the arrival of Buddhism, Tibet's native religion was closely tied to nature. People prayed and gave their allegiance to entities who were not fully enlightened themselves; they were worldly spirits under the sway of their own emotions. Hence, they were easily angered and easily appeased.*

A Strange First Encounter

At the base of the Red Rock mountain of Onphuk, there is a grove of tamarisk trees. Standing under the cool shade of the tamarisks, a twenty-one-year-old Trisong Duetsen and his entourage look eagerly towards the horizon. In the distance, dust hovers in the air. Slowly the cloud of dust moves in closer as the sound of the horses' hoofs and stomping men grows more thunderous. A feeling of nervousness and excitement takes over the Tibetan king as he waits anxiously for Padmasambhava to arrive.

Through the veil of dust, the king tries to apprise the foreigner. As the dust settles down, the visage of Padmasambhava appears, standing next to his horse. Trisong Duetsen comes forward to greet Padmasambhava but because he is the king of Tibet, Trisong Duetsen expects his guest to bow down to him. With his clairvoyant powers, Padmasambhava knows of the king's vanity. He does not bow down, saying to him, 'Listen here, ruler of Tibet! As the bearer of the Buddha's teaching, the king should humbly bow down but it seems your lungs are inflated with your great dominion.' The king's retinue is shocked at the foreigner's disrespect. Padmasambhava continues, 'I will not prostrate to the King of Tibet, but I pay homage to the clothing you wear.' Saying so, he raises one hand in a gesture of homage. Out of the blue, the king's outer garment catches fire. This brings the Tibetan king to his senses. With great appreciation for the master's arrival in Tibet, he immediately prostrates at Padmasambhava's feet.

The Story of the Great Stupa at Boudhanath

In order to understand Padmasambhava's relation with the Tibetans, it is important to go back many lifetimes, prior to his arrival in Tibet. This story is also important as it shows how relations between Tibet and India date back centuries. It is a bond forged even before the birth of the Buddha Shakyamuni and the events thereafter foster the *guru-chela* relationship between Indians and Tibetans.

In the middle of the vast Kathmandu valley in Nepal, one very prominent landmark makes its way into everybody's 'must-see list'. Whether a tourist, a pilgrim or a business person, the Great Stupa at Boudhanath is a must-visit site before one heads back home. The story of how this stupa came about binds the story of Tibet and India as well as the story of Padmasambhava and Tibet.

A long time ago, in the valley of Kathmandu, a poor poultry woman goes to her king to ask for a piece of land to build a stupa. The king grants her request and the construction work commences. Somewhere along the way, the old woman dies. Her three sons take over the job and complete it according to their mother's wishes.

left
Boudhanath Stupa, Boudha, Kathmandu. The most famous landscape in the Kathmandu valley according to the Vajrayana Buddhists. Pilgrims from all over the world visit the Boudhanath Stupa throughout the year. This stupa was built by Padmasambhava, the Tibetan king Trisong Duetsen and the Nalanda abbot Shantarakshita in their previous lives.

In front of the finished stupa, the three sons voice aloud an aspiration. 'May we establish the teachings of the Dharma in the snowy border land.' The first son aspires, 'May I be born as a Dharma king in Tibet, the land of snow, and may I establish the doctrine of the Buddha.' The second son follows, 'When you are a Dharma king, may I be a learned pandit and uphold the doctrine of the Buddha.' Then the third son pronounces, 'When you are born as a Dharma king, may I be a *siddha* invested with magical powers to protect and defend the doctrine of the Buddha.'

Many lifetimes later, these three brothers would be reborn as Shantarakshita of India, Padmasambhava of Uddiyana and Trisong Duetsen of Tibet. Though born in different lands, they would be reunited in Tibet.

The meeting of these three individuals would prove to be of tremendous benefit to the Dharma and to sentient beings. In the land of its birth, Buddhism faced many hurdles which almost led to its extinction, but due to Padmasambhava's arrival in Tibet at the right time, the Buddha Dharma found a safe haven where it not only survived but also flourished. If not for Padmasambhava's work in the snowy land of Tibet, today, we might not have been left with the Vajrayana teachings.

Taming the *Yul-lha*s of Tibet

From atop Mt Hepori, Padmasambhava soars upwards in the air. He looks down into the valley below. The incomplete and wrecked outline of a foundation is visible. In mid-air, he performs the wrathful dance of subjugation. Holding his vajra in the right hand, he communicates, 'Listen! I am the Lotus Born One, untainted by a womb. By experiencing all discursive thoughts to be mind, the threat of terrifying gods and fiends does not intimidate me. The essence of the mind is emptiness beyond concepts, therefore, neither gods nor fiends exist. The enchanting play you display before me will not rouse me even the slightest bit!' He starts performing the ritual of the water *torma*, and by meditative concentration, intensifies it. The *yul-lha*s of the land are told to accept the *torma* offered to them, and in return, they give consent to the use of the land. The *torma* is then hurled into the air.

The *yul-lha*s gather in great numbers, filling the entire valley, mesmerised and magnetised by

Padmasambhava's compelling presence. Padmasambhava continues, 'Gods and Fiends, fulfil the aspiration of Trisong Duetsen.' Performing the wrathful vajra dance of subjugation in the air and chanting wrathfully, 'Hung! Hung! Hung!', Padmasambhava binds the *yul-lha*s under oath and instructs them with directions. As the sun dips behind the mountains, there is a gentle tremor in the earth. From the surrounding mountains, earth and stones roll down into the valley below. Padmasambhava looks towards the mountains and in a great powerful voice, he gives his final order, 'Do not break my command!'

The humans and the non-humans work side by side. What the non-humans build during the night exceeds what the humans build during the day. When there is a shortage of material for the construction, the Nagas come forth with their bountiful treasure and provide Trisong Duetsen with an endless supply of wealth and material. In this way, the construction of the temple proceeds at rapid speed.

It is a time of great happiness for the Tibetan king but the non-Buddhist ministers of the court are not happy. Secretly, they are disappointed that the young king invited foreigners with foreign beliefs to their own land which already has a native faith. There is even a rumour in the palace that Padmasambhava was sent by an Indian king to spy on Tibet and eventually take over Tibet and her vast supply of gold. These ministers are powerful men and they are not willing to lose their influence over the king. They worry that the building of the temple will divert their king's interest away from conquering, and Tibet's imperialistic vision will come to an end.

Turmoil in the King's Court

The princess of the Karchen clan, Yeshe Tsogyal, arrives at Samye as a bride to Trisong Duetsen. Owing to her inclination and faith in the Buddha Dharma, she ran away from home, leaving behind her angry father and enraged suitors who were on the brink of fighting amongst each other. Life was becoming difficult for the chieftain of the Karchen clan and in the end, it was decided that Yeshe Tsogyal be offered to the emperor of the land to prevent further strife. While at Samye, the king

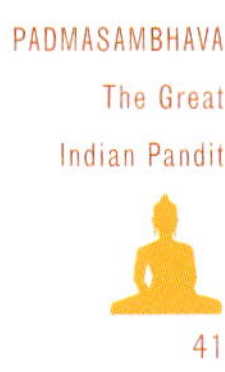

invites Padmasambhava to his palace and offers a vast portion of his domain along with his spiritually inclined queen, Yeshe Tsogyal, displaying the highest form of devotion and non-attachment. The queen, on her part, departs with the Indian yogi with a rejoicing heart.

Around this time, some of the ministers are vocal about their aversion towards the Indian yogi. They talk amongst each other, 'The land is consecrated and Samye is being built but why is Padmasambhava still in Tibet?' They approach the king over this issue, and even go to Padmasambhava and implore him to leave Tibet and her people to its own affairs. In order to soothe and placate the situation and known only to Trisong Duetsen, Padmasambhava, under pretence, decides to go back to India while Shantarakshita oversees the construction of the temple.

On hearing about Padmasambhava's imminent departure from Tibet, the anti-Buddhist ministers are elated. In front of his ministers, Trisong Duetsen bids farewell to Padmasambhava and offers him gold, which the master declines, except for a handful to be offered on the Tibetan king's behalf at the Buddha's Vajra Seat in India. Two of the Buddhist ministers are sent by the king to serve as attendants to Padmasambhava.

As the group advances towards the Nepal border, Padmasambhava with his clairvoyance, sees assassins waiting to ambush them on the way. They have been sent by the zealous ministers to kill Padmasambhava and ensure that he never returns to Tibet. As the assassins lay assault on the group, Padmasambhava lifts his finger and in the mudra of subjugation, he paralyses them.

Arriving at the Gunthang mountain pass, Padmasambhava tells the two Buddhist ministers that he would continue the journey alone thereon. Giving them a handful of *yun-kar* seeds, he instructs the ministers to sprinkle them over the 'frozen' assassins. And then Padmasambhava soars into the sky and disappears. The Buddhist ministers later arrive at the spot where the assassins stood still, and as directed, they sprinkle the seeds over them. The men are brought back to life and news spreads in Tibet that Padmasambhava has left the land.

Yeshe Tsogyal—Padmasambhava's Heart-disciple

Even though in the eyes of the people, Padmasambhava has left Tibet, in actuality, he is very much still in the land and with Yeshe Tsogyal. He teaches her the foundations of the Buddha Dharma and gradually instills in her the importance of spiritual practice in one's life. In her autobiography, Yeshe Tsogyal writes that all the teachings of the Buddha were present in the precious master, Padmasambhava. She goes on to say that all that Padmasambhava possessed, he gave to her, as if pouring water from one vase to another.

In the *Advice from the Lotus Born*, a collection of Padmasambhava's advice to Yeshe Tsogyal, the master tells his student:

'Tsogyal, it is of utmost importance to exert yourself in spiritual practice while you are young. Once you grow old, you may want to listen to teachings but your ears won't hear. You may wish to study, but your attention is dull and your memory fails. You may want to practise, but the strength of the elements has waned and you cannot concentrate. You may want to undertake hardship, but your constitution cannot bear the strain. You will wish, 'If only I had the will when I was young,' but that doesn't help. It is too late to regret not doing any spiritual practice when you are able.'

Yeshe Tsogyal is an emanation of Arya Tara. Arya Tara herself is an emanation of Vajra Varahi and Vajra Varahi is the female Buddha Samantabhadri in reality. She became Padmasambhava's closest confidante and the recipient of all his teachings. Due to her unfailing memory, she could write down all the teachings that she received from Padmasambhava. These were hidden in the form of terma, *treasures to be revealed at a later time in the future. Of all the students of Padmasambhava, she was his heart-disciple.*

More Internal Conflicts

A malicious rumour goes around, claiming that Padmasambhava was not only in Tibet but with the king's consort, that it was the king himself who had offered Yeshe Tsogyal to the foreigner! The non-Buddhist ministers pick up the opportunity to create more obstacles. In their rage, they complain to Trisong Duetsen, 'Give us wise guidance, Lord. Who will guard Tibet if not our local gods!' The

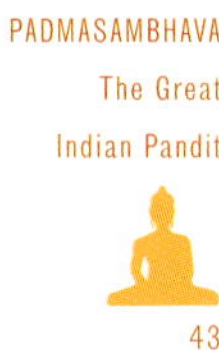

minister Tara Lugong speaks, 'Secretly, the ruler is keeping a black magician whose every word is obeyed. He will destroy Tibet! Lord, you are destroying the law of the kingdom! To run a country, a king needs ministers. If the king feels there is no need for us, then we will retire from our positions.'

Trisong Duetsen is deeply disappointed over his ministers' attitude towards the Dharma and Padmasambhava. Again the ministers appeal to know where their queen is. An infuriated Trisong Duetsen denies knowing anything and the ministers bow down low and take leave of their king.

It is important to know the story of the struggle between the king and some of his court because we then know in what kind of setting the activities of Padmasambhava were being manifested. Even though certain people challenged him personally, Padmasambhava never gave up his compassion for the Tibetan king and his hope for Tibet. If not for him, the Dharma would not have entered the land and the Tibetans would have continued their imperialistic ways. Padmasambhava so to speak 'softened' the Tibetan peoples' hearts with the nectar of the Dharma. That is why this Great Indian Pandit's kindness for Tibet can never be repaid.

In the privacy of his chamber, the king ponders upon the words of his passionately enraged ministers. He wonders how to skillfully respond to the problem facing him and his nation. An elder in his court, Goe, is consulted on this matter. Old Goe advises the king that it is better to be in harmony with his ministers than for Tibet to be broken up and disunited.

Meanwhile, at the cave of Tidro at Zhoto mountain, Padmasambhava discloses to Yeshe Tsogyal, one of the most profound teachings of the Secret Mantra, the mandala of the *Heart Essence of Dakinis,* a profound collection of the Great Perfection teachings. They travel all over Tibet and the Himalayas, consecrating caves, crags and lakes as future sites of retreats for Buddhist practitioners. Padmasambhava himself stays in retreat in these very places, blessing and marking these places by concealing *terma*s for the future, with Yeshe Tsogyal attending diligently.

Samye Monastery

Unknown to the public, Trisong Duetsen and some of the close disciples of Padmasambhava converge at the master's hermitage to receive teachings. Meanwhile, down in the plains of Samye, news travels

fast from one person to the next about Padmasambhava's presence in Tibet. The ministers shake their heads in disbelief and the furrows on the sides of their mouth deepen.

When the news reaches the king's ear, Trisong Duetsen pretends to be genuinely surprised. He makes an announcement saying that if the master was truly in Tibet, then he should be invited to consecrate the finished temple. The non-Buddhist ministers believe that the Indian yogi will never dare show his face again. But they are wrong. As the invitation from the king is sent, Padmasambhava does come to Samye on the day of the consecration.

Under the shade of peacock-feathered parasols, the priest Padmasambhava, the abbot Shantarakshita and the king Trisong Duetsen circumambulate the temple. Suddenly, a shower of the *arura* fruit falls from the skies. An attendant to the king cries out excitedly, 'Your Majesty, it is an *arura*! It must be an auspicious sign!' Two more times, *arura* showers rain over those gathered at Samye and the king is overjoyed. In the courtyard of Samye, the four hounds of copper at the four gates leap into the four directions and bark three times. No sooner do the hounds bark, than the bamboos surrounding the buildings sprout all at once.

Samye holds a special place in the Tibetan peoples' hearts for it was the first Buddhist monastery to be established in the land. It is the source of the Tibetan people's heritage as well as that of the Vajrayana Buddhists all over the world.

Inside the Bodhi temple at Samye, the image of the Buddha Vairochana levitates. Then all the divinities of the main central temple spontaneously come out into the courtyard to greet the priest, the abbot and the king. Trisong Duetsen grows anxious, 'How can we put them back now!' In response, Padmasambhava snaps his fingers and all the divinities go back inside the temple. The sky above Samye fills with vividly manifest male and female Buddhas. The gods and goddesses scatter flowers and a fragrant smell of incense wafts around the temple. Some of the celestial beings sing in the most melodious tune while some play musical instruments. Conches are blown delicately as the divine male and female beings carry the eight auspicious symbols. Down below on earth, at Samye, the men and women who have gathered rejoice over all the miraculous events.

The entire complex of Samye consists of many temples and ritual buildings built in the form of a mandala, the world-system according to ancient Buddhist cosmology. The central and largest temple is built in the form of Mt Meru

Samye takes five years to construct. It is during those years of construction that Padmasambhava explores the whole of Tibet. He gives teachings to the fortunate few and hides many of his teachings as terma *because the time was not right for dissemination; so these* terma*s are 'hidden' to protect them against the ravages of time and to keep them away from alteration, so that the pure and authentic form of Vajrayana teaching exists for the future.*

with two temples on its side, resembling the sun and moon that circle the mythological mountain. Four temples are built to represent the four main continents and eight further temples symbolise the eight subcontinents. Furthermore, many smaller ritual buildings are erected within the complex. The Newari artisans of Nepal along with the Chinese and the Tibetans work side by side, bringing about a unique blend of architecture. The three-storied central temple is designed in the Indian, Chinese and

Samye, Tibet. Samye monastery and its complex of temples. Samye monastery was built in the eighth century and is Tibet's first Buddhist monastery. This is the starting place for the spread of Buddhism and especially that of Vajrayana in Tibet and throughout the world.

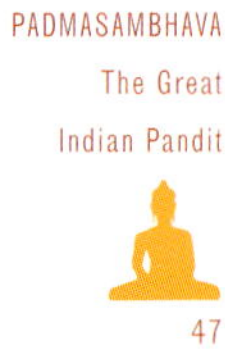

Tibetan styles. Surrounding the entire compound is a gigantic wall crested with magnificent stupas, representing the enlightened mind of the Buddha.

The Dharma Wheel is Set in Motion

After the consecration of Samye, Padmasambhava and Shantarakshita discuss among themselves and express the wish to go back to their lands. They perceive that the people are not ready for the Dharma as the king does not have the backing of his entire court for this noble cause. With the king's wish of establishing the temple fulfilled, the two masters feel that they can now approach the king to discuss their departure.

Trisong Duetsen receives the sad news in great shock. He pleads to them, full of melancholy, 'You have arrived here through the force of your former vows. Although your kindness to Tibet has already been great, please change your intentions. Do not leave me yet!' Saying this, Trisong Duetsen sheds tears, deeply heartbroken. He laments, 'Even though you are disappointed, please anchor the hook of your compassion with us. In this dark land, a Buddha's emanation has arrived whose sole task is for the benefit of all beings.' The sorrowful sight of the weeping king urges both the foreign masters to change their minds.

In order for Tibet to be self-reliant and to have the Dharma flourish in the land, the king is advised to educate young Tibetan boys as translators. Some intelligent boys are brought before the king and the two masters. Shantarakshita tests the children by asking them to repeat the phonetic sound of India after him but the children's pronunciation is nothing like his! The king despairs but Padmasambhava reassures him saying that the Buddha's three main disciples, Ananda, Maudgalputra and Shariputra, are reborn in Tibet. He goes on to say that they will be the first translators who, in turn, will educate more translators. With his wisdom eye, Padmasambhava locates the three boys born into three different families. Trisong Duetsen personally invites the boys to Samye monastery where they are tutored, and they pick up the language of India without difficulty. These earliest *lotsawa*s (translators) were Kawa Paltsek, Chokro Lui Gyaltsen and Jang Yeshe De along with the learned Vairotsana.

The wheel of the Dharma is set in motion with the creation of the sangha of the first seven Tibetan monks at Samye—a monastic tradition of great importance to the flourishing of the practice and teaching of Buddhism. A community of laities practises the Dharma along with the community of monks. Within the gated compound of Samye, among the many different temples and buildings, there are living quarters for the monks, lay male and female practitioners. Amendments are made to the law of the land, in accord with the Dharma. In the entire land of Tibet, the daily life of people is guided by the Ten Virtuous Acts. Under the patronage of Trisong Duetsen, the community of the celibate sangha and the laity practitioners are given support. The king also encourages every household to support the Dharma by being patrons. In this way, in the land of Tibet, the Dharma king, Trisong Duetsen establishes the law of the Buddha Dharma and initiates and popularises the patronage system.

'Though Songtsen Gampo introduced Buddhism to Tibet, because there was no sangha of monks, Buddhism couldn't take a stronghold as it did during Trisong Duetsen's time. Songtsen Gampo had built temples but Samye was Tibet's first monastery. Shantarakshita not only served as its first abbot but because he was a monk whose lineage could be traced to the Buddha himself, with great kindness, he blessed the first seven Tibetan monks.'

Brilliant minded, intelligent Tibetans are enrolled in the translation programme, and while studying the languages, they are also encouraged to study and realise the practices of the Vajrayana teachings. For this purpose, they travel to different parts of India and the subcontinent to study under learned and accomplished masters. Besides braving the heat in India which the Tibetans are not used to, they endure much hardship in reaching these places. One group of the Tibetan *lotsawa*s, headed by the monk Namkhai Nyingpo, goes to the kingdom of Kamarupa in present-day Assam, to study under Padmasambhava's teacher, Master Hungkara. Tibetan translator, Vairotsana and his friend go to India to study under Master Shri Singha, who too, has been a teacher to Padmasambhava.

The hagiography of the lotsawa *Vairotsana describes his travels to India to acquire the teachings of the Secret Mantra. The reader will see how these Tibetans risked their lives for the Dharma and how their Indian counterparts, colleagues and teachers, did their own bit in contributing towards the Dharma. It is because of these people that the teaching of the Vajrayana, the Secret Mantra, still thrives today in its authentic way.*

In India, Buddhism is at its crowning point, attracting the highs and lows of the society. The teachings of the Buddha have created a social revolution among the people as barriers of caste and gender are peeled off. Searching for wisdom within oneself and investigating the spectacular workings of the mind is given prominence over looking outward. It is a time of great enlightenment in *Phag pa yul*—the Land of the Noble Ones—and India has gained a great reputation for being the home of Nalanda and the land of the Buddha. It is also at this time that away from narrow minds, the secret path of the Vajrayana is at its pinnacle. Great siddhas hold some of the greatest secrets to understanding the mind and unlocking its mysteries. It is during the time of Padmasambhava's arrival in Tibet that all these great masters, scholars and siddhas were traversing across the Indian subcontinent.

While teaching the Tibetans, Padmasambhava quotes from the many texts of the Sutra and Tantra. Feeling great necessity for these sutras and tantras to be translated in their entirety, the texts are brought into Tibet without any exclusion. Indian pandits start coming to Tibet on the invitation of Trisong Duetsen to help in the translation of the texts and to expound the Dharma. The first to come to Tibet is Vimalamitra of Western India, followed by more pandits from various parts of the Indian subcontinent, totalling to about 100 learned men. Likewise, 100 Tibetan *lotsawa*s are sent to India to study. There is a flurry of activity over the high passes of the Himalayas as Indians and Tibetans travel back and forth.

When Atisha Dipamkara, the Indian scholar and master from the Vikramashila University, arrived at Samye monastery in the eleventh century, he was amazed at the collection of the Vajrayana literature preserved in Tibet. Most of these Vajrayana texts had disappeared in India by that time. There were also some texts which had never existed earlier in India and Atisha considers these texts to be brought into Tibet by Padmasambhava from the non-human realms of the dakinis *and other pure lands.*

For the pursuit of translation work, a section of Samye monastery is handed over to the Indian pandits and the Tibetan *lotsawa*s. Padmasambhava and Shantarakshita also take part in the translation of the tantras into Tibetan. The *Kangyur*—a collection of Sanskrit classics that trace their origin to the spoken word of the Buddha Shakyamuni—is translated into Tibetan, and the *Tengyur* follows, explaining the books of the *Kangyur*. Translation of the sutras, tantras and their

commentaries progresses at rapid pace as more and more Tibetan *lotsawa*s return from their studies in India. They bring along with them further texts to be translated in Tibet. The pandits and the *lotsawa*s work side by side in translating the Buddha Dharma from the various Indian languages, Uddiyana, Sahor, Kashmir, Singala, Nepal and China.

As the translation work comes to an end, Trisong Duetsen reveres the *lotsawa*s and the pandits, including Padmasambhava, Shantarakshita and Vimalamitra, by showering them with gifts and offering prostrations and circumambulations around them. In this way, the Tibetan king shows his appreciation to the bearers of the Dharma and demonstrates his patronage to the Buddha's teachings in his land.

Padmasambhava's Composition

An outstanding tantra, epitomising all the tantras of the Mahayoga, is the *Guyhagarbha Tantra*, one among those translated at Samye. Great Indian masters like Buddhaguhya, Vilasavajra (Lilavajra, Lalitavajra), Suryaprabhasingha and Padmasambhava have studied the root verse of this tantra and elucidated its meaning in their writings. These are part of the oral lineage, which is transmitted in an unbroken lineage from the masters themselves to the present time.

At Samye, the Guhyagarbha Tantra *was translated from Sanskrit into Tibetan by the* lotsawas *Yeshe Shunu (Jnanakumara, in Sanskrit) and Ma Rinchen Chok, both close disciples of Padmasambhava. In later times, great Tibetan scholars and masters would write their own commentaries based on the Indian commentaries illuminated by the aforementioned Indian masters. One of the great luminaries of Tibetan Buddhism in recent times, Jamgon Mipham (1846-1912), wrote his commentary on this tantra. This tradition of writing commentaries on the tantras finds its source in Padmasambhava and the great pandits of India.*

The rest of Padmasambhava's compositions belong to the *terma* lineage or the direct transmission from Padmasambhava through the revelation of treasure teachings. His compositions take the various forms of aspirations, prayers, advice, sadhanas, pithy instructions, and prophecies, and there are thousands of these compositions available. The works of Padmasambhava have been translated into many different languages for the Vajrayana Buddhists who are now spread all over the world.

Padmasambhava's Plan to Subdue the Ministers

After consecrating the temples built earlier by Songtsen Gampo, Padmasambhava returns to Samye monastery. At the Utse temple in Samye, Padmasambhava expounds the Dharma to the Indian pandits, the Tibetan *lotsawa*s and the master's close disciples. Queen Margyen and some of the ministers, including Tara Lugong and Gyatsa Lhanang, are outraged. Their resentment towards Padmasambhava turns to wrath.

They approach Trisong Duetsen and express their grief. 'My King, we are full of sorrow for much work has been done in an incorrect manner. The ruler has smeared the wealth of the treasury on the mud statues at Samye and elsewhere. How can a king perform his duties without wealth? A king without wealth is a commoner!' Their faces darkened in gloom, the ministers continue, 'You offer affection and warm feelings to the greedy foreigner from the borderland, who lets you squander your life away. In the name of Dharma, strange rules are made and the freedom of the Tibetan people has been taken away. Even the ministers are not taken into consideration and have no authority; our words are given a deaf ear. If this continues, and when enemies come from the outside, what will we do? Will the Dharma vanquish the enemies?' Tara Lugong speaks, 'My king, how can an empire grow when all its men are monks? If the Lord considers the good outcome of the coming together of the ruler and ministers, we should expel Padmasambhava.'

Trisong Duetsen listens to them quietly and his consort Queen Margyen takes her turn. 'Your Majesty, please think carefully. What the ministers say is right. The foreign yogi has stolen the Karchen princess from you and it is possible that he might seize your kingdom. This borderland foreigner is capable of coming in between you and me. How can you trust him? How can a king function without his ministers? You should take heed for the safety of your life. Banish Padmasambhava and let the king and ministers unite in harmony.'

left
Padmasambhava sits on a big multicoloured lotus sprouting from a lake. He is flanked by his female students Yeshe Tsogyal (Tibetan princess) and Mandarava (Indian princess). At the bottom we see the Nalanda abbot Shantarakshita in a red robe and the Tibetan king Trisong Duetsen wearing a white cape.

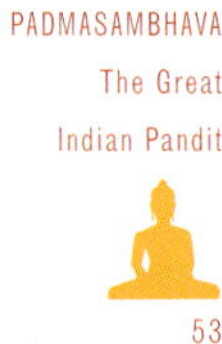

As the sovereign, Trisong Duetsen has to act skillfully, so he tells them that in three days he will have an answer for them. Although he accepts that without ministers, a king cannot rule, he feels disappointed with their attitude towards the Dharma. In the privacy of his chamber, a dejected Trisong Duetsen ponders for a long time. He realises that since Padmasambhava was already at Samye, it might be a wise idea to approach him and get his counsel. With this thought, the king goes to see Padmasambhava and tells him everything.

Padmasambhava responds to the king, 'Great King, we have wisdom and ignorance. Even in the earlier times, whenever a Buddha appeared, a Mara also appeared at the same time. That is why, even during your time, these ministers are Maras in disguise. Wisdom is like the vast sky and ignorance is like the cloud. The cloud cannot impair the sky; likewise, a Mara cannot harm the Buddha's wisdom. The most important thing is that the ruler's mind is firm and anchored, and you have displayed that, and this is an auspicious sign.' Trisong Duetsen is happy with the encouraging words of Padmasambhava.

Padmasambhava continues, 'You should tell the ministers that three days from now, I, Padmasambhava is inviting the *lotsawa*s and the pandits for a celebration at Samye. It will be the perfect opportunity for the ministers to kill all of us but if they do not manage to kill us on that day, then you should tell them that the issue should not be raised before you again.' With their plan in place, Trisong Duetsen takes leave of Padmasambhava.

Miracle at Serkhang Ling Temple

The king summons the ministers and tells them exactly what Padmasambhava has told him to say. The ministers welcome the plot with great delight, their spirits raised.

On a bright early morning, the pandits and the *lotsawa*s gather at the temple of Serkhang ling at Samye. At the same time, outside the main door of the temple, many assassins have assembled. They barge in with their weapons but a great surprise awaits them. No sooner do they enter the prayer hall than all of a sudden, the pandits and the *lotsawa*s transform into statues of Avalokiteshvara.

The assassins are astounded and stare at the inanimate statues with gaping mouths. In the afternoon, more assassins are sent but this time, all the pandits and *lotsawa*s transform into blazing jewels. The men sent by the ministers are seduced by the blazing brilliance of the jewels and the thought of killing escapes their mind.

By evening, the furious ministers themselves lead the assassins and the soldiers. The men burst into the temple chanting, 'Kill! Kill! Kill them all!' At once, Padmasambhava stands up on his throne and uttering, 'Hung! Hung! Hung!' he transforms into a wrathful dark blue deity. All around him, an army of humans and angry gods pervades the whole space. Making wrathful sounds, the miraculous army of gods and humans chase and hunt down the ministers and their minions who scatter in all directions. By a few split seconds, the men manage to step outside the barrier wall of Samye, trembling and gasping for air.

The next morning, Trisong Duetsen sees the ministers and their men sprawled all over the ground outside the wall of Samye. The men have all passed out and their women hover over them, crying their eyes out. Trisong Duetsen is pleased and quickly goes to see Padmasambhava, to describe what he has seen. Giving a handful of earth to the king, Padmasambhava empathetically says, 'We should feel compassion for them. Unless we sprinkle this over them, they will die.' As the earth is sprinkled over the slumbering men, they wake up groggily in a dazed mindset and walk to their homes with unsteady steps.

The non-Buddhist ministers made many plots to kill Padmasambhava but each time he proved them wrong. Through his various acts, both mundane and supramundane, he transformed peoples' perception about the Dharma and instilled in them a change of attitude. For those who were haughty and resilient, he displayed compassion and wisdom through wrathful means of subduing, taming and liberation. Throughout the Indian subcontinent as well as in the land of Tibet, Padmasambhava brought many to spiritual maturity through his compassion. In these different ways, Padmasambhava benefited beings in Tibet and elsewhere.

*Mahasiddha*s of Tibet

One day, while in contemplation, Trisong Duetsen realises that all the teachings that he has received will be of no use if they are not applied in practice. It occurs to him that it is vital for him to request

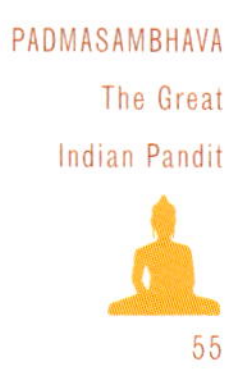

instructions on the Secret Mantra teachings. With this thought, he decides to make the trip up to Chimpu to see Padmasambhava.

At the hermitage of Chimpu, perched high on the mountain, overlooking the valley of Samye, is Padmasambhava's place of retreat. The king arrives at Chimpu with six other students of Padmasambhava. Offering mandalas of gold, they entreat the master, 'Please confer upon us the sadhanas of the Secret Mantra that give enlightenment within one's lifetime.' A delighted Padmasambhava agrees to open the mandala of the *Assemblage of Sugatas*, an important cycle of teachings connected to the Mahayoga Tantra. The Eight *Vidyadhara*s or the Eight Knowledge Holders of the Indian subcontinent transmitted this particular teaching to Padmasambhava, and in turn, he now imparts it to the eight fortunate Tibetans. Upon receiving the empowerments, the eight disciples, including Yeshe Tsogyal, go into retreat to undertake the practice of the individual personal deity conferred upon them.

Each of these eight disciples goes on to demonstrate indications of favourable outcomes in their retreat. Trisong Duetsen can now overpower others' perception of him, the monk Namkhai Nyingpo can travel on the rays of the sun, the yogi Dorje Dudjom can run unobstructed like the wind, the translator Vairotsana can tame and bind the haughty spirits to accomplish his activities, Yeshe Tsogyal can revive the dead, Sangye Yeshe can pierce his ritual dagger into rocks, Gyalwa Choyang can issue out the neigh of the glorious Horse-headed deity Hayagriva and Palgyi Wangchuk gains the perfect confidence of the deity, Vajrakilaya.

Likewise, at many other mountain hermitages including Drak Yerpa, Chuwori, Drak Yangdzong, Yarlung Sheldrak, Yamalung and Zhoto Tidro, Padmasambhava gives instructions and teachings, and bestows upon his disciples empowerments that will lead to their ripening and liberation. These principal disciples came from various backgrounds; some are of royal lineage, some are celibate monks, some are women while some others are yogis or householder practitioners.

Many siddhas emerge from these hermitages; to quote just a few examples—Yeshe Shunu can extract

nectar from dry rock, Yeshe De can fly like a bird in the sky, Pelgi Senge can reverse the flow of a river, Odren Pelgi Wangchuk can move through water like a fish and Ma Rinchen Chok can crush and digest boulders as food. Besides the female disciples Mandarava and Yeshe Tsogyal, there are Shekar Dorje Tso who can walk over water, Melgongza Rinchen Tso who hangs her clothes on the rays of the sun, Chokroza Jangchub Men who can transform her body into fire and water, Zemza Lhamo who, when in need of food or water, can take it from the sky and Rongmenza Tsultrim Dron, who can ingest stones just like food.

At the time of passing away, there are those who dissolve into the body of light and yet others who display rainbow bodies and other miraculous signs of their spiritual maturity. In these myriad ways, the *mahasiddha*s of Tibet, the highly realised male and female disciples, exhibit and display varied signs of accomplishment in their spiritual practice. And throughout the land of Tibet, Padmasambhava makes popular the tradition of mountain hermitages along with the monastic institution of Samye.

The hermitage of Chimpu consists of several caves which were once used as meditation and practice cells by the twenty-five main disciples of Padmasambhava and the master himself. These twenty-five close disciples will go on to become the first mahasiddhas *of Tibet with their miraculous display of power over the mind. Several centuries later, great masters will frequently visit Chimpu and its caves as a place of great blessings. This tradition continues today, where one finds caves dwelled in by lifelong retreatants as also small shacks that dot the entire mountain above Samye. This is an illustration of how Padmasambhava still influences our way of life.*

Terma Tradition of Padmasambhava

Before the passing away of Trisong Duetsen, Padmasambhava prophesies that one of the king's grandsons will destroy the Dharma by multiple means. The king is grief-stricken to hear this but Padmasambhava quickly assures him that he will hide the teachings as *terma*s, which will be revealed at later times by emanations of his chief twenty-five disciples, including the king himself and his sons. Trisong Duetsen is relieved and his hope for the Dharma is not diminished.

Padmasambhava's most important contributions for future generations of Dharma practitioners were concealing a large number of his teachings as terma*—treasure teachings, meant to be revealed at a later time. Even to this day,* termas *are being discovered and revealed by the prophesied Treasure Revealers. During our time, the great master Dilgo Khyentse Rinpoche (twentieth century) revealed many of Padmasambhava's hidden teachings.*

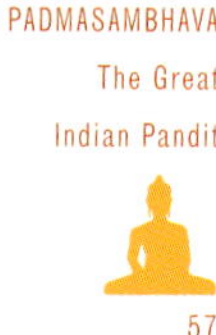

Assisted by Yeshe Tsogyal, Padmasambhava conceals the teachings in a great variety of ways. While concealing them, he makes aspirations and prophecies of their revealers. Padmasambhava transmits these concealed teachings to his heart-disciple Yeshe Tsogyal, and it is she who records them down in different writing styles, including the symbolic language of the *dakini*s. While concealing these teachings in rocks, caves, crags, lakes as well as in space, Padmasambhava would appoint a Dharma Guardian to be the *terdak*, the keeper of the *terma*, until the right person comes along at the auspicious time. This marks the beginning of what is known as the *terma* tradition in Tibet.

Some parts of the story retold here are from the hagiography called The Wish-Fulfilling Tree, *a* terma *revealed by the* terton *Chokgyur Lingpa (nineteenth century). As prophesied by Padmasambhava himself, Chokgyur Lingpa is the reincarnation of the second son of Trisong Duetsen.*

*Terton*s or Treasure Revealers locate the *terma* and bring it to light by practising it themselves first, and at the right time and in the right manner, the teaching of the *terma* is taught publicly, first to the Treasure Revealer's own heart-disciples, and slowly, on a wider scale. Padmasambhava himself in many of his hagiographies lists the names of the *terton*s. Masters having the title *terton (*revealers of concealed treasure teachings) in their name are Padmasambhava's chief disciples who received the transmissions of the *terma* from the master himself and reincarnated hundreds of years later. The sacred teachings taught and concealed by Padmasambhava and Yeshe Tsogyal continue to the present day in the lineage of the *terton*s.

Almost all the hagiographies of Padmasambhava are actually spoken by the master himself and written down while he was in Tibet or after his departure. Yeshe Tsogyal, with her power of unfailing memory, was the chief compiler of Padmasambhava's words. She wrote them down and concealed them as termas *for the future. The retelling of Padmasambhava's life here is gathered from various* termas. *But there are also* namthars, *which are not* terma *in nature, including that of the Tibetan scholar Taranatha (sixteenth/seventeenth century), whose life story of Padmasambhava is based on the oral transmission that he received from his Indian master. Taranatha's master, Buddhagupta-natha, had heard about Padmasambhava from his own guru, Shanti-Gupta.*

right
An image of Padmasambhava carved directly on a rock wall in a small temple at Tashi Ding monastery in West Sikkim. At the bottom we see the Indian princess Mandarava and the Tibetan princess Yeshe Tsogyal. Padmasambhava is very popular among the Buddhists of Sikkim.

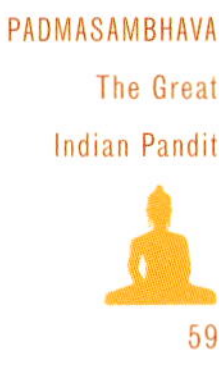

Chamara: The Rakshasa Island of the South-west

At the age of sixty-nine, Trisong Duetsen passes away. Padmasambhava and Shantarakshita enthrone the young son of Trisong Duetsen in a grand ceremony. The new king Mutig Tsenpo is advised to rule the land according to the ways of the Dharma followed by his father, the late king. As the new king stays back at the Red Rock palace, the abbot Shantarakshita travels back to his private residence at Samye and Padmasambhava goes back to Chimpu hermitage.

After some time, news reaches Padmasambhava that Shantarakshita has passed away into nirvana in the Bodhi temple at Samye. Padmasambhava immediately travels down to Samye, and together with the young king, envelops the body of Shantarakshita in the best of silk and prepares it for worship.

Back at his hermitage in Chimpu, while in meditation, Padmasambhava has a vision, a prophecy that was already spoken by the Buddha in the *Sutra of Predictions in Magadha*. In this vision, Padmasambhava sees the rakshasas or cannibal savages of the island of Chamara in the south-west getting ready to spill out into India, Tibet, Nepal and the surrounding lands of the Jambudvipa continent, which is our world. Dressed in their frightening attire of human skin and bones, the demons brandish their weapons of death accompanied by the shrill sound of excitement, as they get ready to flow out of their island.

Tibet's Separation from Padmasambhava

After his vision of the Chamara rakshasas, Padmasambhava visits the young king at Samye and informs him of his need to leave Tibet. The king and the close disciples implore Padmasambhava not to depart but the master tells them that his work through his 'physical presence' for Tibet has come to an end, that it is of utmost importance that he departs soon. Deeply sorrowful, the Tibetan King, Yeshe Tsogyal, the close disciples and the Tibetan public escort Padmasambhava from Samye. The group travels towards Mangyul in southern Tibet.

At the pass of Guntang in Mangyul unfolds the story of the Tibetan people's separation from Padmasambhava. As Padmasambhava speaks, the young king listens attentively, 'The cannibal savages of Chamara are about to spill out of their island into Jambudvipa, bringing about the extinction of the entire human race starting from India, Nepal, Tibet and the neighbouring lands. My time to benefit Tibet in a physical body has come to an end. Besides me, there is no one else to do it, therefore, I need to go to the land of the rakshasas.' The young king, Mutig Tsenpo, is devastated. He feels discouraged for Tibet if the master leaves and he expresses his sorrow to Padmasambhava. 'Trisong Duetsen has passed away. The Guru of Uddiyana departs for the sacred place. Mutig Tsenpo is abandoned in Tibet. The happiness of the Tibetan people has come to an end. Now whom can I trust?' A great cry emanates from the young king and he faints. Padmasambhava quickly revives him and takes the king's head onto his lap. With great compassion in his heart for the young king, Padmasambhava reassures him, 'In reality, I am beyond these concepts. For those with faith, I have never departed. I will still be present for the Tibetan people's need. For those with faith, I will appear in reality and teach. My compassion is swift and has great strength. Do not be distressed, Divine son, ruler of Tibet!'

With a heavy heart Yeshe Tsogyal despondently laments, 'The sun is setting in our hearts. Since you are leaving for Chamara we are left without a guide. What will we do after you leave? What will happen to us? Who do we turn to for advice?' Padmasambhava puts one hand over Yeshe Tsogyal's head and the other on the young king's head.

In a most soothing and compassionate manner Padmasambhava consoles, 'To those who have faith in me, I have never departed. From those with wrong views I am concealed, though yet I stand before them.'

After offering songs of lamentation for the master's departure from Tibet, Padmasambhava gives his parting advice to the king, the ministers, the ordained celibates, the Dharma guides, the yogis and the *tantrika*s, the yoginis and the housewives, the meditators and the patrons, men and women, the healers and the sick, and to the Tibetan people in general. Mounting a beam of sunlight, Padmasambhava in a flicker of a moment,

After Padmasambhava's departure from Tibet, Yeshe Tsogyal, who was his spiritual heir, served as the court priestess. Even though she was in her eighties when Padmasambhava left Tibet, she served the legacy of Padmasambhava by not only guiding the king and many towards enlightenment but also by leading a small team of extraordinary dedicated men in committing to writing the instructions and transmissions which forms the legacy of Padmasambhava.

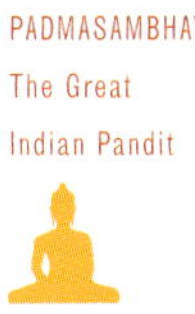

flies away into the sky. From the south-western direction, he turns to look back to the Tibetans one last time, and he speaks, 'Listen to me, Tibetans. I am now leaving. You should also go back now. If you are trapped in the worldly samsara, the seed of Dharma will not sprout within you. Practice the Dharma and follow me.'

And with these words, he sends forth a light ray of immeasurable loving kindness.

If you want to genuinely practise the Dharma, do what is virtuous, in even the most minute deed. Renounce what is evil, in even the tiniest deed. The largest ocean is made from drops of water; even Mount Sumeru and the four continents are made of tiny atoms. The foremost Dharma practice is to keep honesty in thought and deed. The foundation of Dharma practice rests on pure *samaya*, compassion and *bodhichitta*. The *samaya*s of Secret Mantra, the bodhisattva precepts, and the rules of the *shravakas* are all included within this.

Zangdok Palri—The glorious copper-coloured mountain. This is the pure land where Padmasambhava resides in an indestructible body transcending birth and death. This painting was commissioned by the great master Dilgo Khyentse Rinpoche (1910-1991) based on the great *Terton* Chogyur Lingpa's ((1829-1870) vision, who during his lifetime visited the copper-coloured mountain three times during which time he received teachings, transmissions and blessings directly from Padmasambhava.

PADMASAMBHAVA AFTER TIBET

Padmasambhava arrives at the island of rakshasas and subdues the king of the legion of demons. Taking the outer physical form of the rakshasa king, Padmasambhava starts teaching the Buddha Dharma to the inhabitants of Chamara Island.

In the middle of this island is a copper-coloured mountain. On the summit of this mountain, Padmasambhava manifests a magical palace of light called the Lotus Light. To this day, he resides here in an indestructible body transcending birth and death. As long as the ocean of samsara churns, the blessings of Padmasambhava flow without ebbing. He continuously sends out emanations of his body, speech and mind and brings benefits to all beings through the six realms.

left
A wrathful looking Padmasambhava holding a trident in the crook of his left arm. A *kapala* with a vase of longevity sits in this left hand.

right
A shoe print of Padmasambhava.

The Eight Manifestations of Padmasambhava are the eight principal forms assumed by him at different stages in his life. In actuality, they are all the same but appearing and manifesting according to the different needs of the beings.

1. **Padmasambhava**: In connection to his establishing Buddhism in Tibet.

2. **Tsokye Dorje**: In connection to his birth.

3. **Loden Chokse**: In connection to his mastery of the teachings. Padmasambhava would master a teaching the first time he encountered it, and experienced visions of deities without needing to practice.

4. **Pema Gyalpo**: In connection to his kingship. Padmasambhava remained in Uddiyana for thirteen years to teach, as a result of which the king, queen and many others attained realisation and the *rainbow body*. Hence, he was known popularly as Pema Gyalpo, 'The Lotus King'.

5. **Shakya Senge**: In connection to his ordination.

6. **Nyima Ozer**: In connection to his subjugating of demonic spirits and manifesting as a siddha of the charnel grounds.

7. **Senge Dradok**: In connection to his subjugation of non-Buddhists. Padmasambhava challenged and defeated five hundred upholders of wrong views in debate at Bodh Gaya. He reversed their magic with the aid of a wrathful mantra given to him by the lion-faced *dakini* Marajita.

8. **Dorje Drolo**: In connection to his concealing *terma*s and binding the spirits under oath. At thirteen different places bearing the name 'Tiger's Lair', Padmasambhava manifested in the terrifying wrathful form of crazy wisdom, binding worldly spirits under oath to protect the *terma* treasures and to serve the Dharma. Hence, he is popularly known as Dorje Drolo, 'Wild Wrathful Vajra'.

PADMASAMBHAVA

Padmasambhava arrived in Tibet in the Iron Tiger year of 810 AD and left Tibet in the Wood Monkey year of 864 AD. He remained in Tibet for fifty-five years in all—forty-eight years while Trisong Duetsen was alive and seven more years during the reign of Trisong Duetsen's son. This revered Indian pandit tamed one of the fiercest tribes of people inhabiting the highest mountains of the world. Tibetans gave up their warring ways to adopt the more compassionate way of life. Padmasambhava transformed an entire empire, and to this day, his power of influence is great.

One of his simplest and most profound teachings is called 'The Instruction of Pointing the Staff at the Old Man'. While the great master Padmasambhava was staying in Great Rock Hermitage at Samye, Sherab Gyalpo of Ngog, an uneducated sixty-one-year-old man who had the highest faith and strong devotion to the master, served him for one year. All this while Ngog didn't ask for any teachings, nor did the master give him any.

When after a year the master intended to leave, Ngog offered a mandala plate upon which he placed a flower of one ounce of gold. Then he said, Great master, think of me with kindness. First of all, I am uneducated. Second, my intelligence is small. Third, I am old, so my elements are worn down. I beg you to give a teaching to an old man on the verge of death that is simple to understand, can thoroughly cut through doubt, is easy to realise and apply, has an effective view, and will help me in future lives.

The master pointed his walking staff at the old man's heart and gave this instruction: 'Listen here, old man! Look into the awakened mind of your own awareness! It has neither form nor colour, neither centre nor edge. At first, it has no origin but is empty. Next, it has no dwelling place but is empty. At the end, it has no destination but is empty. This emptiness is not made of anything and is clear and cognisant. When you see this and recognise it, you know your natural face. You understand the nature of things. You have then seen the nature of mind, resolved the basic state of reality and cut through doubts about topics of knowledge.

'This awakened mind of awareness is not made out of any material substance; it is self-existing and inherent in yourself. This is the nature of things that is easy to realise because it is not to be sought for elsewhere. This is the nature of mind that does not consist of a concrete perceiver and something perceived to fixate on. It defies the limitations of permanence and annihilation. In it there is nothing to awaken; the awakened state of enlightenment is your own awareness that is naturally awake. In it there is no thing that goes to the hells; awareness is naturally pure. In it there is no practice to carry out; its nature is naturally cognisant. This great view of the natural state is present in yourself: resolve that it is not to be sought for elsewhere.

'When you understand the view in this way and want to apply it in your experience, wherever you stay is the mountain retreat of your body. Whatever external appearance you perceive is a naturally occurring appearance and a naturally empty emptiness; let it be, free from mental constructs.

page 67
A mural of Padmasambhava with the Nalanda abbot Shantarakshita (in a red hat) and the Tibetan king Trisong Duetsen (in a white head wrap). The Indian princess Mandarava and the Tibetan princess Yeshe Tsogyal are seen standing next to Padmasambhava. Below the central figure of Padmasambhava we see his eight manifestations.

Naturally freed appearances become your helpers, and you can practise while taking appearances as the path.

'Within, whatever moves in your mind, whatever you think, has no essence but is empty. Thought occurrences are naturally freed. When remembering your mind essence you can take thoughts as the path and the practice is easy.

'As for the innermost advice: no matter what kind of disturbing emotion you feel, look into the emotion and it tracelessly subsides. The disturbing emotion is thus naturally freed. This is simple to practise.

'When you can practise in this way, your meditation training is not confined to sessions. Knowing that everything is a helper, your meditation experience is unchanging, the innate nature is unceasing, and your conduct is unshackled. Wherever you stay, you are never apart from the innate nature.

'Once you realise this, your material body may be old, but awakened mind doesn't age. It knows no difference between young and old. The innate nature is beyond bias and partiality. When you recognise that awareness, innate wakefulness, is present in yourself, there is no difference between sharp and dull faculties. When you understand that the innate nature, free from bias and partiality, is present in yourself, there is no difference between great and small learning. Even though your body, the support for the mind, falls apart, the *dharmakaya* of awareness wisdom is unceasing. When you gain stability in this unchanging state, there is no difference between a long or short life span.

'Old man, practise the true meaning! Take the practice to heart! Don't mistake words and meaning! Don't part from your friend, diligence! Embrace everything with mindfulness! Don't indulge in idle talk and pointless gossip! Don't become involved in common aims! Don't disturb yourself with the worry of offspring! Don't excessively crave food and drink! Intend to die an ordinary man! Your life is running out, so be diligent! Practise this instruction for an old man on the verge of death!'

Because of pointing the staff at Sherab Gyalpo's heart, this is called 'The Instruction of Pointing the Staff at the Old Man'. Sherab Gyalpo of Ngog was liberated and attained accomplishment.

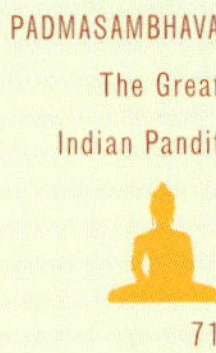

This was written down by the Princess of Kharchen for the sake of future generations. It is known under the name 'The Instruction of Pointing the Staff'.

There are many accounts of Padmasambhava's appearance in Tibet hundreds of years after his departure. He appeared to great masters as well as devoted practitioners in their dreams and in reality. Some have travelled to his pure realm at the copper-coloured mountain, met him there and received transmissions and instructions from him.

No one but an enlightened person can fathom the vastness of another enlightened person's life. If somebody living in the eleventh century was told about the miraculous workings of the iPhone, it would not make sense to him. I have heard that Einstein once said, 'Imagination is more important than knowledge'. Imagination can be understood as being open-minded. Some of the world's greatest discoveries and inventions have emerged as an outcome of being open to myriad possibilities. If the smartest person on this earth, a scholar among scholars, did not have an open mind, he would be limited in his thinking and that would leave no space for further progress and enlightenment.

For anyone, man or woman, who has faith in me, I, the Lotus Born, have never departed—I sleep on their threshold.

—Padmasambhava

GLOSSARY

Arura: In Hindi, it is called Harad, Harada. The scientific name is *Terminalia chebula*. A fruit with medicinal properties used in Ayurveda as well as in Tibetan medicine.

Arya Tara: The female bodhisattva of compassion

Avalokiteshvara: The male bodhisattva of compassion

Bodhichitta: The aspiration to attain liberation/ enlightenment for the sake of all sentient beings.

Bodhisattva: Someone who is endowed with the bodhichitta attitude.

Chamara: It is one of the eight subcontinents surrounding Mt Meru. This island lies to the south-east of Jambudvipa, our world.

Chimpu: The surrounding mountains above Samye monastery which was the hermitage of Padmasambhava and his twenty-five chief disciples. It is still active today.

Chokgyur Lingpa: An important master of the nineteenth century who hails from eastern Tibet. He was the reincarnation of the son of Trisong Duetsen and prophesied by Padmasambhava to be a *terton*.

Dakinis: Extraordinary women of mundane as well as supramundane qualities who are on the path of enlightenment and assist the practitioner on his path. They can also be female deities of the tantra path who protect and serve the Dharma and its adherents. Their male counterpart is called a Daka.

Eight auspicious symbols: *Ashtamangala* in Sanskrit. Each symbol represents an aspect of the Buddha's teaching. The perfect parasol, the auspicious golden fishes, the conch shell of far renown, the perfect lotus bloom, the banner of victory, the wish-fulfilling treasure vase, the wheel of Dharmachakra and the endless knot of infinite wisdom.

Eight worldly concerns: A characteristic of samsara, where one is attached to the concepts of gain, pleasure, praise and fame and dislikes the concepts of loss, pain, blame and bad reputation.

Five Sciences: Grammar, dialectics, healing, arts and crafts, religious philosophy

Great Perfection: *Mahasandhi* in Sanskrit and *Dzogchen* in Tibetan

Hayagriva: The wrathful manifestation of Avalokiteshvara

Heruka: A wrathful deity

Jambudvipa: Our world, which is one of the four continents surrounding Mt Meru according to the Buddhist cosmology.

Kapala: A cup made from a human skull used as a ritual item.

Lotsawa: Tibetan translators

Mahasiddha: Great adept

Mahotarra: Also called *Chemchok* in Tibetan. This deity embodies all the enlightened qualities of the Buddha.

Mandala: *Kyil khor* in Tibetan, directly translates as 'centre and surrounding'.
1. Can be a deity along with its retinue. It is also the visual representation of the tantric deity's realm.
2. A mandala offering is an offering visualisation of the entire universe as well as material offering.

Mudra: Gesture

Nagas: Guardians of great wealth and treasures who inhabit water bodies

Pandits: The masters of the Indian subcontinent who came to Tibet to assist in the expounding and propagation of the Dharma.

Sadhana: A guide or manual on how to accomplish a particular practice.

Samantabhadri: The mother of all the Buddhas of the three times. Her male counterpart is called Samantabhadra.

Samsara: The cycle of birth, death and rebirth within the six realms of existence marked by suffering, impermanence and ignorance.

Six realms: Realm of celestial gods, demigods, humans, animals, hungry ghosts and hell beings

Stupa: A structure in the shape of a semi-hemispherical dome, it houses Buddhist relics and represents the enlightened mind of the Buddha. The Tibetan 'chorten' and the 'pagodas' of the Asian countries are also stupas.

Ten Virtuous Acts: To avoid the three physical misdeeds of killing, stealing and sexual misconduct. To avoid the four verbal misdeeds of lying, harsh speech, slander and idle gossip. To avoid the three mental misdeeds of desire, harbouring ill feeling and having wrong views.

Terdak: The guardian of a *terma* appointed by Padmasambhava to guard the *terma* until the coming of the destined *terton*.

Terma: The treasures and teachings concealed by Padmasambhava.

Terton: The revealer of the *terma*. *Terton*s are prophesied by Padmasambhava himself.

Three Jewels: The Buddha, the Dharma and the Sangha

Tibet: A popular name for Tibet is the Land of Snow because of its location atop the Himalayas.

Torma: Ritual cake or offering (Balim, in Sanskrit)

Tirthikas: Adherents of the extremist views

Vajra: 'Dorjee' in Tibetan. It describes the qualities of unconquerable, impregnable, indestructible. It is also a ritual implement.

Vajra Seat: The place where prince Siddhartha sat down to meditate and awoke as the enlightened Buddha. It is in present-day Bodh Gaya.

Vajrakilaya: *Phur ba* in Tibetan. The deity is the wrathful form of Vajrasattva.

Vishuddha: *Yangdak* in Tibetan. This deity is the wrathful manifestation of Vajrapani.

Vajravarahi: A wisdom *dakini* with a sow's head protruding above her left ear. She is the wrathful form of the *dakini* Vajrayogini. She is the queen of the fierce *dakini*s.

Yamantaka: The wrathful manifestation of Manjushri

Yul-lhas: Native gods and spirits of Tibet

Yun-kar seed: Mustard seeds

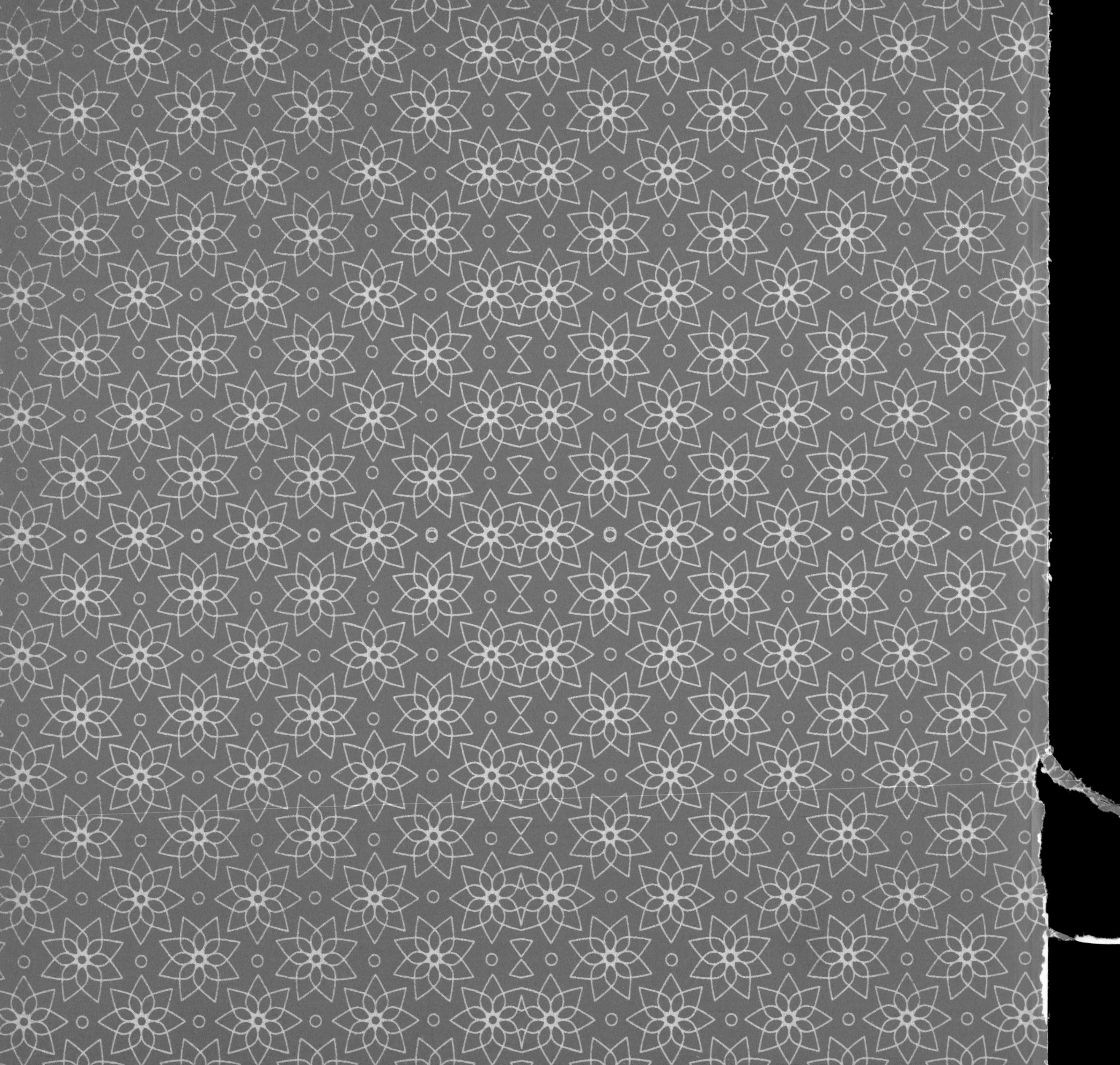